Educating for Right-Action and Love: Extending and Expanding the Montessori Vision

Phil's discovery of Montessori, which taught him that "Montessori is not merely a method of education but a spiritual approach to life that has the potential to change the way human beings live – from self-centred, material values to altruism, peace, and collaboration" – proved to be a life-changing event, eventually leading to the foundation of TIES, where Phil and his wife Marsha developed their own special brand of "Montessori for adults."

Because of his interest in the education of adolescents and Cosmic Education, during the 1970s Phil contacted Mario Montessori Jr., which not only resulted in an enduring friendship with the Montessori family but also in fulfilling Phil's quest for the roots and authenticity of Montessori. Phil's motto: All good things in all good time is certainly applicable to this wonderful book published at the right time.

Carolina Montessori
Montessori author and historian

Madam Montessori was a pioneer who altered the whole vision of education with a holistic approach that integrated Science, Philosophy, Psychology and Religion. The methods she evolved were informed by this new spirit of education which she enunciated. In this book Dr. Gang has extended that vision, spirit and approach to address contemporary problems facing modern society and shown that these require a fundamental transformation of human consciousness which such education can undertake. This book shows how education can create a new global mind and a society with peace, justice and happiness for all.

P. Krishna, Ph.D.
Author of *A Jewel on a Silver Platter: Remembering Krishnamurti*
Member of Krishnamurti Foundation India and the Theosophical Society
Lecturer on education, science, and spirituality

Using his own life as a portal, Dr. Gang guides us into a vast and exhilarating landscape of profound insights, each one revealing yet another that inspires and moves us to deeper love and alignment with the whole. Montessorians will be gobsmacked with how this book reveals whole new layers of Montessori's work, particularly during the years in India. She stuns us even now. (How the heck did she come up with all of this back in the 1930s and '40s?) This book will have a prominent place on my reference shelf where I can regularly revisit the quotes, ideas, and more for many years to come.

Jennifer Morgan, President, Deeptime Network
Author, *Born With a Bang: The Universe Tells Our Cosmic Story*,
From Lava to Life: The Universe Tells Our Earth Story
and *Mammals Who Morph: The Universe Tells Our Evolution Story*

The greatest teachers are co-learners. They are questioners, and they sometimes defiantly challenge convention in their search for truth. They teach not only with words, but by the example of their lives. Phil Gang gives us the gift of such a life well-lived, but also teaches us the art of the deeper, well-asked questions that define our better natures. His lifetime of living the questions has opened a portal to freedom beyond the conditioning that restrains us as human beings. Education for Right-Action and Love is by turns poetic and personal, then visionary and universal. It combines the warmth and intimacy of a memoir with a powerful roadmap for connecting us to Gaia and Cosmos. This is the rich and culture-changing teaching deeply needed in education and life today. Phil writes about his life as "exploring a river of influences and confluences" and of envisioning "the Great River" on a cosmic scale. Jump in. Be swept away by its stream of wisdom, compassion, and transformation.

Lauren de Boer, MA
Essayist, poet, and composer specializing in nature, spirit, and the human imagination.

Phil Gang has created a deeply transformative communion with the divine by incarnating spirit and spiritual approaches in his written word.

John Fowler, Ph.D.
Developer of the Time Line of Light

This book's narrative invites readers to glimpse into a beautiful tapestry, embedded with pearls of wisdom and diamonds of inspiration. It weaves together the legacy of remarkable educators with the writer's exceptional life journey, illustrating the genesis of the essence of holistic teaching and transformative learning. Read closely to unearth a treasure – a blueprint for integrative curricula, pedagogy, processes, and contexts – all ingredients for the core principles of the education of the future.

Nimrod Sheinman, B.Sc., N.D.
Founder, Israel's Center for Mind-Body Medicine
Founder, the International Soul of Education Initiative

The wisdom enfolded in this book is a golden chariot that will not only carry you across the cosmos, it will deliver you to the door of your true home in the Universe. May it inspire you, as the TIES program inspired me, to seek and embody your soul's burning question as a sacred offering to The Great Work of our times.

Edveeje Fairchild, M.Ed.
Founding Chief Operations Officer of TreeSisters,
Founder of A Woman's Nature School

Dr. Gang's book, *Educating for Right Action and Love* is magical, profound and endearing. He combines his biography with the history of the Montessori movement, his own educational insights and so much more. Using the metaphor of a river, he invites the reader to follow the course of the development of his heart as well as his thought. With many references to Montessori's works, Eastern thought as well as dynamic ecological, Gaia thinkers, his book is like taking a course in life. He proposes more than a few things worth thinking about.

Mary Ellen Maunz M.Ed.
Author of *Nurturing Your Child's Inner Life*,
Director of Montessori Training at Age of Montessori

Educating for Right-Action and Love is Gang's response to important questions inspired by and tethered to three great women in his life, Ruth Gloria, Marsha Snow Morgan, and Maria Montessori. Through this great work, educators have an opportunity to learn how to create environments that support freedom of choice in an atmosphere where learners and educators mutually embrace right-action and love. This work is an important contribution to all educators and to the field of holistic education.

Josette Luvmour, Ph.D.
Adjunct Faculty, Antioch University
Author of *Growing Together: Parenting as
a Path to Well-being, Wisdom and Joy*

Written by Montessori family friend and historian Philip Gang, this book weaves a tapestry of story that integrates the author's life journey as seeker and teacher with Maria Montessori's spiritual legacy. This is an essential work for educators, as well as anyone wishing to understand integrative learning as key to the betterment of oneself, and humanity.

Delila Olsson, M.Ed.
Montessori School Director

Philip Snow Gang has woven the remarkable adventures of his life into a readable map for the future of educational thinking. He puts Dr. Maria Montessori into a context that utilizes the wisdom of those who have come before and after her time. He uses his intelligence, experiences and reflective capacities to invite us to deepen our understanding of the human task before us and accept it with Love.

Mary Raudonis Loew
Montessori Teacher Trainer and Consultant

Philip Snow Gang's personal and professional journey reflect a life-long devotion to Montessori's vision for a new education that leads to the emergence of a new human. Emerging through Gang's practical experiences, research, and reflections, this book provides a deep comprehension of Cosmic Education for children and adults. Dr. Gang shares his journey through a historical context that includes communications and references to those who were close to Maria Montessori. Reading this book will accelerate your spiritual preparation as an educator and help you understand why it is necessary for humanity to connect to the Cosmos as a way into lifelong transformation.

Claudia Langlois, M.Ed.
President - Canadian Association of Montessori Teachers

A stunningly beautiful book from a Montessori-education pioneer…part memoir, part science book, part 21st century Universe story. But mostly, this is a living story of how the Montessori approach to education might hasten the evolution of what author Phil Gang calls the "new humans" – future generations with radically different ideas about the meaning of the human experiment. This book could not have come at a better time.

Terry O'Keefe
Business Writer

I am struck by how poetically the book weaves together these mind-boggling concepts about nature and universe, yet does so in a way that is grounded in sensorial detail, gratitude and love which makes it accessible in a way that simple facts would not.

Rachael Jaimeson, MFA
Poet and Mindfulness Educator

A hero's journey
offering deep insight and gratitude
in poetic form
to the Universe and Gaia
with Montessori's cosmic vision felt and understood;
guiding humanity
to transform, inspire, integrate, educate
for Right-Action and Love.

Betsy Coe, Ph.D,
Director of Houston Montessori Center
Montessori pioneer of adolescent programs

I read *Educating for Right-Action and Love* with awe, the poetry of the words, which comes from the depths of life itself.

Shubha Narayan
Co-Director, Nova Montessori School

While reading *Educating for Right-Action and Love,* I was acutely aware of the deep listening one experiences in that timeless place of attention when one is not separate from the word. As travelers wave to each other, never to meet again, I noticed how the words disappeared and the perfume of that meeting and the deep essence of those words remained with me, in my heart, in my soul and in my actions. We were no longer strangers, we were one.

Pauline Matsis
Co-Founder and Co-Director, Nova Montessori School

EDUCATING FOR RIGHT-ACTION AND LOVE

Extending and Expanding the Montessori Vision

Philip Snow Gang

with Tamara Castleman

Dagaz Press

Dagaz Press
Portland, Oregon, USA

Dagaz Press is the publication branch of The Institute for Educational Studies (TIES)

Copyright © 2020 Philip Snow Gang

The poem by Ed Edmo©2006 is printed with permission of the author. All rights reserved.

Cataloging-in-Publication Data for this title is available from the Library of Congress

ISBN 978-1-09833-970-8 (print)
ISBN 978-1-09833-971-5 (ebook)

1.Education 2. Montessori 3. Memoir 4. Spirituality/Consciousness

10 9 8 7 6 5 4 3 2 1

This book was typeset in Adobe Garamond

To send correspondence to the author of this book contact him through
https://www.philipsnowgang.net

Dedicated to my wife and soulmate, Marsha Snow Morgan (1943-2017),
whose love and wisdom helped inform this book

and for my grandchildren:
Perth Silvers
Dylan and Jordan Moliken

GRATITUDES

There have been so many people in my life who have directly contributed to the evolution and writing of this book. Some of the "influencers" have been identified throughout the writing. These acknowledgements, however, are for those individuals and places that made this project possible. While it is true that in many ways this book has been a lifetime in the creating, it began to coalesce in earnest nine years ago during my 2011 lectures in Brazil. To tackle a project as large as this one requires people in your life who provide a safe place and space. For this I have so much gratitude to my daughter, Sharon, and son-in-love, Warren, who not only provided this safety, but also took over all of my administrative responsibilities directing the graduate programs at The Institute for Educational Studies (TIES). I could not have embraced, much less completed, a project of this scope without their amazing support during the years of transition from living in New Zealand and caretaking for my wife, to the huge shift of back to the United States and the evolution of a shared residence.

Tamara Castleman raised her hand immediately when I decided to put this lifetime journey in writing. In fact, her continuous prodding, "You have to write this, Phil, there's no one else who knows the story," gave me the momentum to continue the process, even when things got tough. She helped, not only with inspiration, but also by helping me flesh out ideas that were missing and identifying those things better left unsaid. The truth is, without Tamara's guidance, this book would not be what it is.

As the writing process unfolded, a renewed long-time kinship with the Montessori family flowered. Carolina Montessori (Maria Montessori's great-granddaughter) and I had lost contact soon after her father's death, but our friendship never waned. I have so much gratitude for her being a dear friend and an immediate and reliable resource for my basket of questions about what Montessori said and where she said it.

A year before Ralph Metzner passed away, I spent a day with this colleague of 30 years near Muir Woods outside of San Francisco. At one point, after I had explained my understanding of the spiritual essence of Maria Montessori's ideas, he said to me as clear as a bell, "*You* have to write the story."

I offer much gratitude to John Fowler, who was always standing by to dialogue about my latest philosophical insight or perspective. His vast knowledge and interest in these matters enabled my writing to be more translucent. Along with John, the other TIES faculty – Kathryn Ross, Julie Haagenson, Steven Arnold, Linda Engelhart, and Paul Freedman – have contributed to the realizations in Chapter Eleven, which like all things, evolved over time. And I acknowledge the TIES students and graduates who have informed my vision for tertiary education.

I thank all those who read all or portions of the manuscript, Delila Olsson, Terry O'Keefe, Warren Gang, Shubha Narayan, Pauline Matsis, and Rebecca Jaimeson. Rebecca had a very strong influence as I learned the art of mindful writing under her guidance.

Throughout the early stages of this writing I was inspired by the sessions I had with energy worker and intuitive, Katie Todd, which helped me see into portals of understanding that eventually flowed into poetry and words. Katie is also an artist and, based on my work with her, created the painting that is now the cover of this book.

Appreciation is offered to all those writers and thinkers who paved the way for my understanding and love for Cosmos and Gaia.

And finally, I extend my deepest gratitude to the trees – especially Grandmother Red Cedar – and other beings at Tryon Creek State Park (Portland, Oregon) as well as the sand hills and ocean at the beach adjacent to my home in Christchurch, New Zealand. They offered me inspiration and grounding.

CONTENTS

FOREWORD

From a very early age, my children had a seemingly innate sense of what is "right" in a given situation. Not only that, but they have always known what they do not know, never in a sense of "No one's told me," but, rather, in a way that says, "I haven't learned that for myself yet." I wish I could say that my parenting was always stunningly robust, but I am a typical parent, for better or worse. I wish I could say that I was blessed with somewhat magical children, but they, too, were typical, if a truly typical child is to be found. What then made the difference? From my perspective, it was the Montessori education they received from ages 3 and 4 through third grade.

In the Montessori realm, my daughter's learning disabilities were non-issues, not non-existent, but simply something to be worked through, and the materials offered to her allowed her to learn without much teacher support needed. It wasn't until we made our foray into public school that we were told she had a "problem." Also new to us in public school was that nature walks weren't part of the curriculum, that children were given no choice over what they learned or for how long, that while individual teachers cared deeply about students, they, too, were hamstrung by a corporate system that had no place for right-action and allowed little room for love to blossom.

Although I am a product of public education, I was dismayed to see that it fundamentally had not changed in the decades I'd been away from it. I wanted to know more about what made Montessori work so beautifully that children were allowed 90 minutes of time outside every day when the public schools around me were cutting recess to as little 15 minutes to gain more instructional time. Something worked in Montessori that wasn't happening in other settings, and I was more than a little intrigued.

I enrolled as a graduate student with The Institute for Educational Studies (TIES) through Endicott College to obtain a Masters in Education with an emphasis in Montessori Integrative Learning. The program assigns each student a mentor and Phil Gang was selected to be mine. At the time I had no idea of Phil's background – that he had at that time been a major player in the world of Montessori and holistic education for over 40 years, that he has abiding friendships with the Montessori family beginning with Mario Montessori, Sr., and continuing with Maria Montessori's great-granddaughter, Carolina, today, or that he had lectured extensively throughout the world. To me, he was simply Phil, Academic Dean, and the person who read my papers.

I also did not realize that as a student I would have the wonderful opportunity to learn in a Montessori way. As part of my field work, I spent a great deal of time in a 6-9 (1st-3rd grade) classroom and was cured of a lifelong math phobia simply by working with the materials as a child would. I came into TIES with definite ideas about everything, because good students have definite ideas – better to be definite and wrong then tentative in any way, right? No, I learned. Tentative was not weak, it was a sign of strength to be able to admit that you might not know. I have come to believe that being tentative is the first step toward right-action: This seems wrong to me, can we brainstorm ideas for fixing it together? When there is love, it is easy to be tentative. Right-action grows from love. During my tenure at TIES, I had what would have been some pretty spectacular failures in a conventional educational environment. Phil just said, "All good things in all good time," meaning I was learning, and he was confident I would eventually understand. I never worked harder in my life, but it was fun, and by the end I did understand. I have not been the same since.

You are holding a treasure in your hands. Phil Gang is the only person I know who has the knowledge, the connections, the education, and the personal experiences to write this book, a book that I believe extends and expands the Montessori vision as it promises. I have been utterly amazed by the insights in this book and am so grateful they are in print to share with you. My fondest wish is that all people experience education as right-action growing out of love. May it be so for you, too, dear reader.

Tamara Castleman, 2020

PROLOGUE

". . . the consciousness we have is simply a filtering down of some form of universal consciousness." — Aldous Huxley [1]

"Love is conceded to humans as a gift that is directed for a certain purpose and a special reason and, in that, it resembles everything lent to human beings by the cosmic consciousness." — Maria Montessori [2]

Inspiration has been present in my life. She appears at intervals reminding me that there is an alternate side to explore, a new venture to undertake, a new intimacy with truth revealed, or a conditioned way of being that needs to change.

As I reflect upon my past, I see those moments as energetic times that have refocused my direction. In the early '70s, my two children were enrolled in a Montessori school, which led to a series of events that completely altered my future. I had been a manufacturing engineer working for a large military contractor. Despite job and financial success, I felt like a stranger in a strange world. This feeling was not new to me as it was quite dominant throughout my schooling and in my family. I never felt like I "fit in" with my peers. I was not part of the dominant paradigm, but I didn't know it.

Something happened to me during my visits to the Montessori school. There was a unique energy and exchange that I had never experienced before. It made me feel like whatever I was looking for in the world was real. The compassion, caring, and love was visible at a feeling level. At the time I did not realize I was having a spiritual experience. As my contacts with teachers increased, I came to understand the meaning of "kindred spirit." Their way of sharing the Montessori approach was inspirational and I began to feel a stronger identity with Montessori ideals. It was a philosophy that deeply resonated with me; so much so, that I remember the day that I pulled over onto the freeway shoulder on my way home from work in order to ponder how different my life would have been had I been educated like this.

Inspiration came and sat next to me during the summer of 1973 while I was having a conversation with my son's teacher, Don Jenny. Without precognition I said "One day I might like to be a Montessori teacher." I was surprised by the power of the words as they came out of my mouth. Don, nonchalantly replied, "Why not now?" At that moment I felt an inner burst of light circulate in my body, finding its way to my heart. I couldn't speak. Finally I just laughed, and laughed... and laughed. A few days later I set the intention to travel to Bergamo, Italy with my family for the Montessori yearlong course of study. Joseph Campbell says that the hero hears the call to adventure and makes a decision to separate from the current reality.

Inspiration followed me throughout my time as a Montessori teacher, head of school, and international conference organizer. She then sat next to me in the late '80s when I made the decision to move on, without knowing what I was moving on to.

Subsequently I founded the Global Alliance for Transforming Education (GATE) and then the Institute for Educational Studies (TIES) Master of Education programs in Montessori Integrative Learning and Integrative Learning. In the midst of these creative forces, Inspiration invited me into dynamic cosmic love with Marsha Morgan who became my loving and intellectual partner for the rest of her life.

What is the source of Inspiration? Where does she come from and why has she been such a frequent visitor?

Questions like these have been at the forefront of my thinking in recent times. Perhaps it is because at my age I can look back and view the people and events that were present throughout my life at strategic moments and recognize them as catalysts for a deeper exploration of the Ground, the transcendent and the immanent. I know that Inspiration does not come out of the void but springs forward in the journey of the self toward the Self.

This book is the story of my own journey and how it has led me to believe that educating for right-action and love has the potential to create a transformative shift in the way we care for each other and the Earth community as a whole.

In my 1989 book, *Rethinking Education,* I explored 20th century scientific revelations in quantum and relativity physics in order to articulate one emerging theme – the unity principle – that everything in the Universe is interconnected and interdependent. I posited that understanding this would be primary to the development of holistic education. What has evolved for me over the last 30 years is a deeper realization that you cannot prepare holistic education teachers in a non-holistic way. You cannot prepare Montessori teachers in a non-Montessori way.

Despite my wife's deteriorating Alzheimer's condition and subsequent passing, Inspiration has been beside me for the last seven years as I was determined to articulate what we had learned and created together. The results of this exploration will be found woven into this book.

Since 1996 TIES has been working with graduate learners online in a Montessori way. Interestingly, we did not set this as an intention, but I will explain later how we have accomplished this.

My hope is that readers will experience how one question can arise in your life and, living into that question may be your soul's calling.

PART ONE:
EMERGENCE

CHAPTER ONE:
THE QUESTION

Be patient toward all that is unsolved in your heart and . . . try to
love the questions themselves like locked rooms and like books
that are written in a foreign tongue. Do not seek the answers,
which cannot be given you because you would not be able to live
them. And the point is, to live everything. Live the questions now.
Perhaps you will then gradually, without noticing it, live along
some distant day into the answer.

It is also good to love: because love is difficult. For one human being
to love another human being: that is perhaps the most difficult task
that has been entrusted to us, the ultimate task, the final test and
proof, the work for which all other work is merely preparation.
R. M. Rilke[3]

In the spring of 2017, I took my two teenaged granddaughters, Dylan and
Jordan, to Europe on a perfectly designed and wonderful holiday that turned to
custard after the first week. I was excited to show them Paris and the places in
Italy that made their grandfather a Montessori teacher, but the lingering shadow
of my best friend and intellectual partner, my beautiful wife and soulmate,
Marsha Morgan, was so present that I was an emotional wasteland and could
not travel on to Italy after that first week in Paris. Everything, every airport

transition, every gallery, brought back memories of holding Marsha's hand as we walked the streets and museums of Paris. Perhaps I had a premonition that she would, after living with Alzheimer's for seven years, leave her body within two months. Our trip was cut short, and I came home an internal shambles, wondering whether I, who had so easily traveled the world and lived in other countries, could ever manage travel beyond my neighborhood again.

Remarkable growth and healing took place in the year after I lost Marsha to Alzheimer's and – with our friend, Rhonda – released her ashes into a Rocky Mountain stream, Colorado always having been Marsha's spiritual home. I intentionally resumed my lifelong passion for long walks in the forest, something my grandson, Perth, informed me is called *forest bathing,* but to me has always been how I reclaim my center. I started taking Tai Chi classes, which meet outdoors, no matter what the weather is here in Oregon, where I currently live.

Throughout these years I maintained my work as Academic Dean and Program Director with the TIES M.Ed. programs that Marsha and I founded in 1996. As explained in the Prologue, TIES applies Montessori philosophy and principles with adult learners, who choose their own emphasis area in either Integrated Learning or Montessori Integrated Learning. I also started writing in earnest. The week before Marsha died, I discovered a workshop in mindful writing, which engages writing as a meditation technique. In mindful writing one uses prompts to stimulate the flow of ideas. The writing is timed. For anywhere from ten to twenty minutes, I keep my hand moving on paper. Without time to think or reflect, doubt is assuaged and ideas flow from the center of my being. Not only did I enjoy this practice, I found that I had much to say. Suddenly poetry was pouring from my pen. Ideas that had been stored inside my physical body were appearing to my eyes on paper, revealing streams of consciousness, expressing a synthesis of my inner and outer journey throughout my entire life. At the end of a writing session I would often ask myself, "Where did these words come from?" I began to see writing as a spiritual practice observing my life's journey unfold in written form at the end of my pen.

These life experiences ultimately have led to the formation of a driving question that explores educating for the future of humanity. "Right-education… and Love" are the objective, but how do we get there? What is the contextual framework? As I was writing the script for *To Educate Eco-Sapiens* (see Chapter Ten) all of a sudden the question appeared without thought and onto the paper. When that question came into clear focus, I knew immediately that in order for someone to join me in its exploration, that person needed the benefit of understanding the seeds that were sown during my life and how they germinated into, first the roots of the question, and then the answers and responses themselves.

The time had come to write this book, to share my story, my experiences, and the answers, as I understand them. That much I understood. What I wasn't sure of was how I was going to take on such a big project without Marsha's help. She was my champion and my stability point. She was also an incredibly talented, gifted, and loving person who understood my vision better than I did at times. Certainly she could eloquently articulate it with me. We danced the most beautiful cosmic waltz together, and the music stopped far too soon for either of our liking. During our years together our ideas became as intertwined as our lives. Sometimes it is difficult to remember what was mine alone, Marsha's alone, or ours together. Within that lies a primal paradox: the tension between one's drive to be an individual and the drive to collaborate with others.

Some days I hear the music and have no partner. Some days I dance alone. Still, I feel Marsha's prodding from the next plane, saying, "Go do *The Work*." I decided to heed her intensions and move forward with what are you reading, but first, I had to return to Italy. I still owed Dylan and Jordan a trip, and I needed to prove to myself that I could still travel. I needed to return to my birthplace.

Yes, I grew up in Queens, New York, but I feel like I was born in Bergamo, Italy, when I left that job in engineering and uprooted my first wife and our children from our Atlanta, Georgia home to become a Montessori teacher. In

1973, Bergamo was the only place in the world to become certified to work with ages six through twelve. When I deeply studied and understood the comprehensive Montessori philosophy, I came alive. It was for me a rebirth; Marsha expressed similar feelings when she did her coursework there in 1970-1971.

This time I planned my trip to Italy with the family much more carefully. I arranged to go ahead of my granddaughters so that I could have a week in Stockholm with old friends in order to rest and adjust to the time change. I also knew I needed some solitary time because that had become holy territory for me. I invited my daughter and son-in-love to accompany my granddaughters, and when they arrived I was well-rested and good in health and spirits. We went back and visited the Bergamo Centre where I studied, as well as the Montessori school my daughter, Sharon, had attended. Sharon enjoyed reminiscing about her own memories of living in Italy as a child, while their family had the opportunity to explore the things that interested them, which left me with much free, alone-time to roam and wander – just what the cosmic doctor ordered.

Before I left the States, I was overcome with a sense that I needed to leave some sort of memorial in Bergamo for Marsha. Marsha and I completed training at different times, met some years later, and then didn't become romantically involved for decades. Sometimes true cosmic love takes a very long time to blossom.

Leaving just a few of her ashes seemed most fitting, but by then they had already incorporated themselves into that gorgeous Colorado stream. It never occurred to me to save some for later; they, like Marsha, always belonged to the Earth. Perhaps, then, I could leave a bit of her personal writing. Yes, that made sense to me, but I also wanted to leave a personal belonging, something that could be given as a gift to someone else, something that would entice the person to read the words. This was not a habit of ours, to leave little gifts behind for others. This was Inspiration speaking to me.

I chose a butterfly brooch that Marsha was fond of wearing. It was gold and covered in dark, muted rhinestones. Marsha was simple in her tastes. The brooch was small and understated, but it sparkled when she wore it as though it had come alive itself because she was so in touch with Gaia and all that our planet offers. I photocopied some thoughts she had written on index cards in her perfect penmanship. Here is an excerpt containing some of the words written on those index cards that I was now ready to pass on.

> Are the children always the change point of evolution? The next incarnation of collective wisdom? They will be conditioned for benefit or woe by what we provide. The atmosphere must be imbued with the attitudes, convictions, and values that invite human flowering. The content must mirror the wonder of discoveries of what has gone before and covet skills for discovering more as well as the ability to express.
>
> We shall not create a world full of academic botanists or even a large contingent of avid gardeners. That need not even be our mission but we provide a space of wonder of observation. At the very least we have shown a light through a window filled with inter-connectedness . . .

I left the brooch attached to the writing in the corner of the doorway of the now unoccupied apartment building where Marsha had lived during her time studying in Bergamo. I have a picture taken in that doorway shortly before we ended our final visit to Bergamo in 2012, and you can see in her eyes that she is reluctant to leave home, as we all are when the nest has long been declared closed and we know in our hearts we will never be returning. It felt ceremonial to me as I walked up and lovingly placed my offering with a little prayer that someone would find it and pass it on because I was passing on our love for each other, this world, the children, our planet, Gaia and Cosmos. I took some pictures for my own memories and walked away with a light heart. I had no doubt that my offering and Marsha's gift would be gone by the next day, and I was not disappointed when I stopped at the doorway to check. Where it ended up is fodder for the imagination but ultimately irrelevant. All that matters is that it was taken.

When Marsha became ill, there was a moment during my caretaking that she turned to me and said "You do not need this in your life; go do The Work." I cared for her at home as long as I could, and then the time came when I had to do as she instructed. Marsha, in her great love and passionate wisdom insisted that I be free, demanding that I carry on our Great Work. In her passing, watching her fill a stream with essence and become part of it, knowing that somewhere in Italy a gold and rhinestone butterfly is soaring, I have been able to at last free her as well.

Now, I am ready to delve with you into the deeper questions of right-education and some of the possible responses I have experienced over a long and adventurous life.

A driving question is both as simple and complex as it sounds as it reveals a single question that drives all other inquiry in hopes of establishing a context for an all-encompassing exploration. It's simple because many questions are inherently simple: Who? What? Where? When? Why? Why not? Questions are what make us human. Even our earliest human ancestors, without language, would have used questioning gestures to clarify situations. However, a driving question is more philosophical and often resolves into other questions like spokes on a wheel. Asked in a provocative way, it will most assuredly have more than one possible response and most likely has no one "correct" answer. Conventional thinking and education tend to make people search for the *correct* answer, sitting with only the possibility of what might be "right."

When a driving question summarizes a lifetime of work, one may be tempted to think of the questioner pondering late at night or in the wee hours of the morning, tinkering with thought for years to come up with a single idea that expresses a lifetime of observing and learning. I suppose it does happen that way for some scientists, but more often, I think that the question suddenly emerges fully formed, like Athena springing from the head of Zeus. Rather apt that the goddess of wisdom sprung fully formed from her father's head, because in my case, that is what happened with my driving question. It came from the ethers where soul spoke to me.

I have spent the majority of my adult life opening doors of possibility while educating with children and adults. Quite often I ask leading queries in hopes of helping students discover their own driving questions. The process of developing questions "worth thinking about" was primary during the years of my relationship with Marsha. In fact, in order to understand what was happening at the very beginning of our time together we drew a Mind Map titled "What does it mean to be in transition?" The map drew out 24 contextual questions. We saw no need to seek answers for each question, knowing that the questions were enough.

I honestly hadn't thought much about whether or not I had a driving question of my own. However, approaching my late seventies, I did begin to spend more time reflecting on my legacy. Over the last few years I began wondering how I might articulate what I had integrated over nearly 50 years of teaching and learning with people of all ages, and I wondered if there was some way to summarize the work that Marsha and I had created together. I did not, however, sit in the forest and ponder sage-like, trying to distill these thoughts. I let wisdom be my guide.

In 2015, I was asked by the Deep Time Journey Network to create a presentation for a 2016 series of webinars. At the time I did not know that it would develop into a film, and I had no idea until it was finished that the work would reveal the core nature of Integrative Learning, and insight into the graduate program that Marsha and I developed through TIES. Nowadays students study the film during the last semester of that Master's program. Writing the script (see Chapter Ten) was one of those exercises where the words flowed faster than I could get them on paper. I was scribe for the Universe and the Universe was dictating quickly. And this was before I came upon mindful writing. One typically rainy Northwest Pacific day, I looked down at my paper and there was my driving question, every word perfect:

What contexts and processes in education

might liberate teachers and learners

so that they become

catalysts for a new human,

one whose integral relationship with Gaia

is bound by Right-Action and Love?

I was gobsmacked! No matter that something has been brewing for 50 years, when it appears in front of you fully formed, it's a wonderful, magical surprise. And then you are left having to respond. What continues to amaze me is that several years later the question remains as it is without revision. That is unusual in my experience. I am sure today that there was no better way I could express my explorations, as the question became part of the air I breathe.

My very next questions, the spokes on the wheel, were: *What people and experiences in my own life have been catalysts for the emergence of this question? How did this question come to form within me? Why now, when most people my age are enjoying their grandchildren and their hobbies? Why me, when I no longer have my intellectual partner to join me in playing tennis with these ideas? Why me, and if not me, then whom? Why me?*

And then the Vedic concept of Indra's Net appeared again in my life. In the early 2000s Marsha first discovered the poetic verse on the back of a box of chai tea. She shared it with me and thought we should post it on campus to provide insight into words written thousands of years ago that some might say "predicted" emerging possibilities for communication via the Internet. It was not until recently that I discovered notes from a book I read in 1991 that addressed the same verse. In *The Quantum Self* author and speaker Danah Zohar explains that according to the Buddhist Diamond Sutra:

In the house of Indra there is said to be a network of pearls so arranged that if you look at one you will see all the others reflected in it. In the same way, each object in the world is not merely itself but involves every other object, and in fact, is every other object. [4]

Sometimes cosmic wisdom is vast and glorious and sometimes it's on the back of a cardboard tea caddy.

The story of Indra's Net stayed in the back of my mind for years. When my driving question appeared, I was prompted to go back into Vedic literature and find it again. According to the story, Indra, the god of heaven, has a net of infinite dimension. The horizontal threads that make up the fabric are space. The vertical threads are time. At each intersection where time and space meet, there is a crystal bead. You are one of those beads. So am I. Every single life form, all forms of consciousness in the Universe that ever was or currently is, is a crystal bead, and every time a being is born a new crystal is added to the net. If you get close enough to an individual bead, you will see that it shines in a way that allows it to reflect every other bead in the entire net. We are all interconnected within time and space. When you find you have a shared experience with someone even though you grew up 30 years and 3,000 miles apart, that is Indra's Net reflecting itself back to you. It also means that nothing separates you from another being. You have your own spot on the Net that belongs to you and you alone, but your function within Indra's Net is to reflect every other crystal that shares the infinite space with you.

The idea of Indra's Net is not out of keeping with our current understanding of quantum physics. My lifelong interest in science is evident in old family movies that show six-year old Philip conducting some sort of experiment with Mason jars full of soil on my grandparents' New Jersey farm. To the casual observer, those films probably look like a young boy playing in dirt, but I knew that I was making important discoveries about the natural world. As my formal education continued, I became fascinated by astronomy and big questions. I did not know the word yet, but I was interested in cosmology. It's probably not surprising, then, that before I turned to education, I decided to become an engineer. (Although my importance was taken down a peg when, at 17, I told my 88-year-old grandmother that I intended to study engineering and she responded that running trains wasn't a bad way to make a living.)

As my interest in cosmology grew, so did my interest in ecology and an understanding of Gaia Theory. It was fortuitous when I met Marsha and our collaboration began in earnest because she was fascinated by cosmology and had a deep understanding of ecology. I was fascinated by ecology and had an abiding interest in cosmology and quantum physics. We became a perfect Yin/Yang as we learned from each other and blended what we knew, an ideal meshing of the reflection of our crystal beads on Indra's Net.

I invite you to join me on this personal exploration of my driving question and offer these definitions of the terms of the question:

Contexts. Context refers to the content and story that one needs to understand in order to make learning relevant. One might picture a series of concentric circles with the new learning as the innermost circle and each successive outer circle embracing what one needs to know in order to situate the inner circle. For me everything is a derivative of the outer circle – the Universe Story.

Processes. Processes are verbs – the way in which learners engage content. Before educating became my focus, I thought that if people were given contextualized content, right-action would emerge. Now I know for sure that the process – the way teachers work with learners – must be congruent with content. Years ago I wrote, "You cannot teach democracy using nondemocratic means." A process-orientation for learning is equally relevant to children and adult learners.

Liberate. Liberation is a process of releasing cultural conditioning so that one can be aware and attuned to the presence and potential of now. It involves awareness of conditioning as well as the power of observation to immediately release previously held assumptions. The process of liberation nourishes the spiritual evolution of humanity and the rise of a new human.

Catalysts. In the context of this exploration catalysts are teachers and learners who are on the journey of liberation, both individually and collectively.

New Human. Liberated teachers and learners are the roots and seedling for the New Human. Indian philosopher Jiddu Krishnamurti explains, "It is becoming more and more obvious and necessary that through a different kind of education a new human being comes into being."[5] In *Education and Peace*, Maria Montessori writes "The new human being must show us how to make all humankind aware of its unity"[6] and in *Education for a New World* she points to "the rising of a New Human who will not be the victim of events, but will have the clarity of vision to direct and shape the future of human society."[7]

Gaia. Gaia theory describes Earth as a totally integrated living system. All the living and nonliving components of the biosphere work together in a massive interconnected and interdependent network, just like the crystal beads described by Indra's Net some 3,000 years ago. Native people and mystics throughout time did not need science to prove this; they experienced it directly by living intimately with the natural world. Today, knowledge of systemic integration is imperative for the future of life on Earth.

Right-Action. Right-Action takes place when one responds with integrity to the flow/unity of life and being. It is a response to "what-is" and free from conditioning.

Love. Love is the attraction to otherness that permeates the Universe and expresses itself in beauty. Loving awareness is the human quality that embraces the spark of creation in every form – the crystal bead that is and reflects every other crystal bead in Indra's Net. In *The Absorbent Mind*, Montessori writes:

Love is no other than one aspect of a very complex universal
force, which – denoted by the words "attraction" and "affinity" – rules the world, keeps the stars in their courses, causes
the conjunction of atoms to form new substances and holds
things down on Earth's surface. It is the force that regulates
and orders the organic and inorganic, which becomes incorporated into the essence of everything and all things, like
a guide to salvation and to the endlessness of evolution. It
is generally unconscious, but in life it sometimes assumes
consciousness, and, when felt in [the human heart] heart, [it
is called] "love."[8]

When I was about eight, I decided I wanted to plant a peach tree. My
grandfather had been a baker all his life, but retired as a farmer, so I asked him
to help me. He said that the soil was mostly clay, and he wasn't at all sure a
peach tree would take root in that soil, but it couldn't hurt to try. He helped me
plant a few peach pits, and I waited. One of them did take. It grew big enough
and strong enough for me to transplant it. When we moved from one part of
Queens to another, it was still small enough that I was able to take it with me.
Not too many years after that, it started bearing fruit, and our housekeeper,
Ruth Gloria, would make the most delicious sugar-free peach pies I've ever
had. Recently I realized that the peach tree my grandfather helped me plant was
something I held as a metaphor for my life and cosmological understanding. I
have been transplanted: New York to Georgia to Italy to Vermont to California
to New Zealand to Oregon with countless mini-stops in between, and each
time I have grown stronger for the move. My life has born tremendous fruit,
including a family I love, work that makes me feel like I am contributing,
opportunities to open doors of possibility to students of all ages, as well as
time for introspection, walks in the forest and making furniture – all the time
reflecting as much of Indra's Net back as I am able.

A tree is also an excellent metaphor because the roots, my earliest
experiences and the people who first reflected Indra's Net back to me, were

foundational to my journey. The trunk holds the ideas, events, and experiences that led the Universe to provide the driving question in the first place. The branches are my exploration of possible responses to the driving question. This book is designed to follow that same pattern. I will introduce my foundational experiences, the ideas and events that grew into the trunk of my thinking, and then share the fruit of my ideas found on the branches. The book can certainly be read sequentially, but the intention is that you can turn to any chapter and find a juicy peach waiting for you.

What if, instead of one right answer, there is a plethora of possibilities? What if you were allowed, encouraged in fact, to reflect Indra's Net back to itself, to reflect your essence in my crystal bead in the manner that made sense for what and whom you were created to be? How freeing would it be to allow all of Indra's Net to be reflected in the bead that is you without restriction, without a right answer? Our current model of conventional education has placed too much emphasis on the "right way" and "best outcomes" without stopping to ask, "What liberates teachers and learners to be who they have been created to be? How do we engage children so that Right-Action and Love are natural by-products of being alive, not skills that are somehow taught? Couldn't that sort of education be a catalyst for a new human? A happier, healthier human in right relation with Gaia and his or her fellow inhabitants on Indra's Net?"

In sixth grade, I had a wonderful teacher named Mrs. Noguera who had us start every day reading the newspaper. Somehow the day flowed naturally from there and we covered all the subject material seamlessly and joyfully. It seemed how one was supposed to learn, and I felt free. In the middle of that year, my family moved to a new neighborhood, which meant a change of schools, and my teacher was the meanest and worst I'd ever had. Mrs. Noguera had shown me what education could be; I could barely believe I was expected to endure this. Too often we think that children don't understand what is possible, but from my observation, they know whether they're being treated fairly. They can't always articulate what isn't quite right, but they can tell you whether they like a teacher, and much has to do with how the teacher manages learning.

The children can always tell you. I knew at a soul level that my first sixth grade teacher was wonderful and my second shouldn't have been a teacher at all.

This book explores the potential humanity has to create a benevolent and sustainable future for the rise of the new Earth community. Seen through the lens of my experience, I will share the essence of what I have learned about integrative learning as a way forward through an education whose principles and processes empower the current generation to create that benevolent and sustainable future. I will focus on educating, but I hope by now it is clear that it goes far deeper. Right-Action. Love. Integral relationships with Gaia. New humans. Catalysts. Liberation. This book is written for anyone who is interested in exploring the questions. Will you join me in eating a peach?

CHAPTER TWO:
ROOTS

To be one with cosmos
and one with self
in sustained
moments of grace.

During this eighth year of my eighth decade I search for essence; I am wakening to the realization that previously invisible connecting threads are now discernible, enabling me to see my roots and influences as ripples creating the contexts and processes that have danced me through life. At the moment they occurred, these intersections with people as well as events and experiences were not predictive of an unfolding context. It is only the awareness of today that reveals the context in formation, and how that tapestry created a meaningful matrix of knowing based on *seeing*, as Gregory Bateson said, "the patterns that connect."[9]

When others say "You have to tell the story; share the vision," I ask, "Why me?" Rewinding my personal timeline, I see how opportunities presented themselves and, despite the fear of the unknown, I had the courage, hope, and inspiration to engage creative responses to rising situations. I now see how these responses were guided by Love... that Love that emanates from All that is.

For some 50 years my life has been enriched through teaching and learning with children and adults. Like Indra's Net, my personal story and my work in education are indivisible. Something stirred inside me from as far back as I can remember. There was definitely an awareness that I was living in a two-dimensional world of yes-no, right-wrong, good-bad. Just when I thought I understood the game, I discovered that the rules changed. What I thought was right might be wrong the next time. Conversely what I thought was wrong might be appropriate the next time. Though I aspired to be like them, the adults in my life bewildered me. Both family and teachers responded without questioning and without pause, from an "automated space," what I now understand as the conditioned mind.

During my youth there were, however, a few adults that were unique, so unique that it took me decades to begin to understand their influence. Ruth Gloria Hope was our live-in housekeeper. Her presence allowed me to validate that there was more to living than what I had experienced. Why did I feel "I don't belong here?" Why did I feel like I needed protection? Everything changed with Ruth Gloria's arrival. Until she crossed my path, God was an abstraction: a ritual here and there and a synagogue gathering twice a year. I had no awareness of something beyond the self. Ruth was part of a large ministry of people who followed the guidance of their spiritual leader, Father Divine. From the 1920s through the 1960s he was a proponent of peace and global cooperation in the black community. In a 1950 letter to my parents he wrote, "We truly represent and live and produce that Peace that surpasses all human understanding."

Not all of his followers were like Ruth. Her predecessor, Joyful, was neither joyful nor peaceful. In fact, she was often quite cruel. When I was seven years old, I arrived home after school one day, and she would not let me out to play with my friends. I went into a rage and jumped out the kitchen window into the garden, a full story down. A chipped front tooth still reminds me of this escape. Metaphorically, maybe learning how to jump without a net was a huge gift in disguise as it prepared me for later professional and personal jumps.

On rare occasions, Ruth took me to her home and church on Sundays. I had never been inside a church, let alone an all black congregation singing and dancing prayers and glory to their God. I was swept into another zone. Gospel was way different than my parents' opera or the Frank Sinatra my sister listened to. I was so moved by that sound that I rose from my seat and, clapping my hands with everyone else, began dancing in the aisles with the other children and adults, parading around the auditorium. It must have looked odd to see one white face in a sea of black and brown.

I also remember being introduced to Father Divine. His soft charisma viscerally brought Spirit into my nine-year-old awareness. "Peace Ruth" was both my greeting and salutation as she never used the words "hello" or "good-bye." So, peace was constantly in my vocabulary, and became a strong root and context throughout my life.

The memories of her relationship to the plant world are indelible. God was definitely in Ruth's garden. She would spend free time either sewing or taking care of plants. I watched her propagate seeds for flowers and vegetables, observing how she cared for and loved them. I can see her now with garden hose in hand giving pansies a bath in our front yard. Inside the house she would wipe leaves of plants with a milk-dampened cloth, and actually drop into a conversation with them. I thought it strange, but at the same time I was captivated by her personal dialogue with the plant world. I started my first vegetable garden as a teenager and have tried to continue that ritual throughout my life.

Ruth also had a disquieting side and was subject to mood swings and outright despair. I have vivid memories of trying to coax her out of being absent. I knocked on her door pleading for her to sew something for me that was urgently needed. And sometimes that worked.

When Ruth went "missing" I felt like my *protection* went missing. I recall an incident when, to the chagrin of my parents, I had made a very strong and challenging assertion. In the background I heard Ruth whispering, "and the little child shall lead them." Those words are embedded in another thread made visible – a root established at a young age that was revealed with my involvement in Montessori education. Maria Montessori is known to have told her followers: "Do not follow me, follow the child as your guide."

In the mid-1950s there was civil unrest in the Southern States where white people were rallying against school desegregation. Growing up in New York, it was easy for me as a teenager attending a 95% white high school to shake my finger at the South. Later I would learn that school districts in northern cities were sometimes carved out to prevent mixing of race and class. Segregation news really disturbed Ruth. I saw it in her eyes as I observed her reaction to the massive unrest. When a huge hurricane ripped through many of the cities where people had been advocating "segregation now, segregation forever," the storm left a path of destruction, and I distinctly remember Ruth saying, "God works mysterious ways." My right-action context for civil and human rights emerged during these tumultuous years. Later in life, as an education advocate, I was honored to meet and have relationships with such luminaries as Andrew Young, Ralph David Abernathy, and Hosea Williams.

There was another event with Ruth that I have rarely shared. I was 14. Ruth notified my parents she was leaving, quitting, and returning home. She had given this warning before, but she always changed her mind. This time she packed her bags, called a taxi and was ready to go back to her home on Halleck Street in Newark, New Jersey. Hat on head, coat on back, she was at the bottom of the stairs with my mother when I realized, "This was it!"

I panicked. It would take something unprecedented for her to stay. I walked down the first flight of steps in our split-level home and then faked a fall down the second set of stairs, whining from a potential injury. This got their attention as they both hovered over me. To this day, I am sure this act helped to change Ruth's mind.

"Saving Philip from the dominant reality" required her presence for the rest of my adolescence. What might have terrified me about losing Ruth? She assuaged the feelings I had about being that "fish out of water." I needed her love, her deep devotion to life to lift me up when I got stuck in the world of disharmony. When I graduated from the eighth grade she wrote in my autograph book:

Success. Health. Prosperity

As you go through life's pathway

ask God for an understanding heart

So that Peace and Happiness

may be yours always.

Ruth Gloria.

In the late '70s I received a handwritten letter from a sister in Ruth's community telling me that she had passed on. At the moment of death she was holding a picture of my son, Warren, and daughter, Sharon. Her last words were "My children, my babies."

Experiences with Ruth Gloria sowed early seeds for personal spiritual exploration, understanding Gaia, right-action, and the education of children. I still feel her presence, especially on forest walks when I sometimes see her smiling and saying, "You are having a good life."

Universal love

manifested in my life

when an Angel appeared

in real time

and she was there

to guide me in spirit.

Cosmos allowed me to

drink from her

spiritual perspective

— a disciple of Father Divine

a poignant figure

in the black liberation

surge during the 1920s, '30s and '40s.

A man who created

an international peace movement
a man who called himself
God
who probably didn't know the word guru
whose hands I touched
whose voice I heard
whose music I danced to
in the aisles of
Ruth Gloria's church
one Sunday
when I was nine years old

My mother says my sister was "born that way." What way? Sad, no smile, unhappy, whiny. Although she was eight years my elder, I do not recall many moments where she expressed joy. Fear was present; fear of school, fear of new places, and fear of going to social events: "Where am I going to sit? Whose table? I don't want to sit with them. Why are they putting me with children?" Oddly, no fear of driving; she pressed onwards despite opposition.

I wanted her to be happier – especially at meals. Sitting down to dinner was always unpredictable. If Ruthie was upset or had a sad face, my father's patience was thin. "I work hard all day and don't want to come home to *this*. What's wrong with you?" If she did not respond he might say, "Leave the table and come back when you can smile." I felt awful for my sister because my dad's fury was inescapable. At the same time, I may have thought "Glad I'm the good one." I was so torn.

She left the table, and I followed soon after. I knocked on her door; she let me in. I tried to diminish her angst by rubbing her back or lightly tickling her arm. She returned to dinner. I was 12 or 13.

Episodes of Ruthie being abused came into my awareness when I was much younger. Like the time she was tied with ropes by peers, including some cousins. She was dragged on the gravel road; there were cuts on her back and burn marks on her body for proof. Why did such a thing happen? I wanted revenge. But what could a five-year-old do? Today I realize they must have ridiculed her because she was uncoordinated and could not run, jump, and play like the others; slow and immature in thought; highly stressed at school and home; dowdy and frumpy.

The psychiatrist, of all people, should have seen the truth. My sister did not experience the world in the same way as other people her age. She had limited capacities. She was a misfit in ordinary education and had to go to a private high school to learn office filing-skills.

When Ruthie was 60, Marsha met her for the first time. After a few days Marsha speculated that my sister is on the autism spectrum. Although there are ways that she was adaptive, she had limited capacity for reflective thinking and could easily go into a tantrum when she was frustrated. At the same time, she could play the piano merely by listening to music on the radio and, without reading notes, find the melody with her right hand and replicate the music using both hands. She also had excellent drawing skills and a beautiful handwriting. Everything fell into place and I finally see her life in a whole different way. I imagine her as a child thriving in a Montessori environment. Why wasn't she praised for her incredible music skills? Did the psychiatrist know that she could play the piano or that she could draw and write with a degree of skill?

On one of my visits back home, I looked at photographs in the family album and my mother said, "See, Ruthie never smiled." When I was a child I recall thinking, "This takes all the pressure off of me." My parents were also not very happy with my brother, Danny, who was 14 years older than I. He wanted to be an auto mechanic and chose the wrong wife, marrying into the wrong family.

After two disappointments, here came Philip: strong-willed, cunning, creative, memorized entire books before he could read and clearly had a mathematical mind. Finally, my parents had a child that would match Aunt Dora's three prodigies. Aunt Dora was 10 years older than my mother and the matriarch of the family. In fact, she was a much stronger influence on my mom than their mother. Aunt Dora and my mother had a binding relationship that caused me many grievances, but that is another story.

I was my parents' favorite …and I loved that role …until I got caught …doing something they labeled "bad" …when, in my innocence …I was unaware of naughty …I was just being Philip. My mother's response might be, "You'll get yours." What did that mean? It gave me the message that I had gotten away with something this time, but I would eventually be caught. Even when I was declared exempt from the draft there was a sarcastic "You'll get yours someday." These memories help me understand how important it was for me later in life to explore and work within a system that liberates children and adults from conditioning.

When my mother was not out playing cards or mahjong, there was time for affection. It found its way to me through her hands and heart. I was her baby and, much to my embarrassment and consternation, she usually introduced me as such. This image of "baby" enabled her tender, mothering side to emerge. She would often rub my back, even when I was a teenager.

My mother was quite protective of me when my father unleashed his displeasure and disbelief at my behavior. When he went over the edge, she would speak in Yiddish, something that sounded like "luzimup." I only knew very few Yiddish words; the tone of this phrase made me think she was saying, "Love him up." However, now I know that *luzim* means "let him," so maybe she was saying, *"Let him be."*

My sister never left home. The tension was always there. As an adult I could feel it when I walked into the house after a long absence. What do I take away from how my sister's life influenced my directions? Those family experiences fostered the emergence of compassion and understanding as well as a strong sensitivity to women's feelings.

My earliest memory of anything "scientific" was a metal erector set complete with lattices, nuts and bolts, and pulleys. My cousin Paul lived down the street and he taught me how to take pictures and develop them in his darkroom. I became a budding chemist and photographer.

When I was 11 years old my teacher, Mrs. Noguera, introduced us to integrative learning. She did not give her process that name; TIES was one of the first to name it as a degree some 50 years later. Noguera's classroom was a beacon of interdisciplinary activity from one "subject" to the next in a seamless sequence.

Three years later during my first year in high school we were required to take a year-long course in general science. General Science was a composite of biology, Earth science, chemistry, and physics. George Schwartz was not only a high school teacher, but also appeared weekly as "Mr. Science" on a local TV program. His classroom was a beehive of activity, applying what we were studying in books. It was quintessentially experiential. In Mr. Schwartz's class I completed a research on photography and made a pinhole camera that actually worked. I took and developed several images. That camera and those photographs were placed on display in the science department showcase. During the 12th grade I made a glass pyramid for Solid Geometry demonstrating how to compute its volume. These two experiences planted the seeds for my understanding of the importance of experiential learning.

Unfortunately, those were my only good takeaways from high school. My classmate, and well-known vocalist, Paul Simon, in the first two lines of his song, *Kodachrome*, sings about the insignificance of what he learned in high school.[10]

I was also very interested in astronomy during high school and remember buying a book about stars, as astronomy was not a covered "subject." However, the book I remember the most was one titled *Philosophers of Science*. I recall it began by exploring the work of Lucretius. His "De Rerum Natura" (On the Nature of Things) was an epic contribution to thinking in ancient Greece. The scientific worldview helped me look deeper into mystery, not just science, but also responding to questions like: *Where did we come from? What is the meaning of life? Why are we here?* These thoughts were for inner reflection as there was no one amongst my peers or in my adult world with whom I could have this conversation. It is apparent to me now that my interest in science helped me begin to explore the greater contexts that embrace these questions. I am sure that my passion for exploring origins has been a response to my own need to situate *Who I am* and *Why I am here* in a greater context.

From kindergarten through university there were three teachers – Mrs. Noguera in elementary school, Mr. Schwartz in high school, and then Claude Rainey at University – who made meaningful contributions to my life. Rainey appeared as the typical-looking 1950's Professor of English: tweed jacket, bow tie, bald, and horn-rimmed glasses. Beneath those accouterments he was animated and philosophical, which was quite extraordinary at an engineering school. I signed up for an elective in English just so I could be in his presence again. I remember visiting him in his office and talking about life, not about the course I was taking, but about how to live life. He said something startling to me as I described what I perceived as mind-limiting and authoritarian gestures coming from my parents. "Fuck them. You are your own person." I was taken by surprise, first by the source and then noticing the release I felt. It was the first opportunity I had to look at my own conditioning: that I could do what I wanted in the world according to my own journey.

Revisiting my early years, I see defiance on one hand and sensitivity on the other. How did that contribute to my life's work? Insight emerges. I now realize that these two attributes were some of the roots that have enabled me to embrace an education for children and adults that allows them to be who they are. It is a way of being-learning that is in stark contrast to the dominant industrial-corporate model. It is a way of creating learning environments for children and adults that is sensitive to their needs and based on inherent human tendencies.

In 1900, Nettie and Morris Gang emigrated from Iasi, Romania. Three years later, their first of six children, my father, George, was born in Brooklyn, New York. My grandfather Morris was a well-known woodcarver in the old country, but at the turn of the 20th century people wanted things "machine made," so he was never able to support his family. Six children lived in a one-room tenement, four girls on one mattress and the two boys on the other. My father was quite proud that he attended 13 different elementary schools; it did not matter that the cause of their mobility was my grandfather's inability to find work. My dad loved telling me two stories that revealed this poverty.

The cost of going to a "talkie" at the moving picture show was three cents each or two for five cents. He would stand in front saying, "I got two, whose got three?" Inside mothers would leave babies in carriages in the lobby of movie theaters. A number was placed on the carriage and if the baby awoke, someone would walk across the stage saying, "Baby in carriage number 5 is crying." Another story was about jellybeans. Each Saturday he would take his younger siblings and cousins to the silent movies. His mother and aunt alternated giving him 25 cents each week. One week they doubled up and he went to Woolworth's with his newfound wealth and bought 25 cents worth of jellybeans. You can imagine how much that weighed in 1915! They all got sick… so sick, that my father never ate a jellybean for the rest of his life.

In 1888 my mother's parents emigrated from what was then Austro-Hungary; Grandma Anna's homeland is today's Poland while Grandpa Isaac's is Ukraine. I have traced the Snow lineage back to the birth of my great-great grandfather, Eleazar Wolf in 1796. He lived in the forests of the Carpathian Mountains and owned a sawmill. So, on both the Gang and Snow sides wood and forests dominated their lives. Nowadays I think I may have inherited that meme, which is the reason I make furniture.

My mother, Fannie, was their fifth of six surviving children. By the time she was born the family was financially stable as Isaac's bakery apprenticeship in Lvov (Lemberg when under German control; Lviv, today) enabled him to secure employment in Brooklyn and to eventually open his own bakery.

My parents grew up within a 10-minute walk from each other's home in the Williamsburg section of Brooklyn but did not meet until they were adults. In fact my father's parents shopped in my mother's parents' bakery.

Grandchild of immigrants, I am only one step away from an old country and old customs – customs that my grandparents would maintain without the history that came with them. They never shared stories of what their old lives were like, but they brought their customs and mannerisms with them. My parents grew up in two paradigms; they were Yiddish-speaking children of Eastern European immigrants as well as new Americans trying to fit in and leave the old mannerisms behind.

Embedded in a dominant Judaic culture, I sometimes think I am a refugee from Woody Allen's *Annie Hall*, complete with Klezmer music. We engaged in all the traditional holidays; there was a sense of belonging, but I was never sure "what" I belonged to. I was sent to Hebrew school and had a rather meaningful bar mitzvah, not so much for spiritual awakening, but for the personal accomplishment and recognition that came my way. In the eyes of others, I had done exceedingly well.

My own spiritual journey would not take root under the roof of organized religion.

My mother's singular measure of success was monetary accumulation. "Look how well so and so is doing." It did not matter what so and so did as long as he was a financial success. My father pushed himself to measure up to her standards, so when bankruptcy hit at age 60, he rarely smiled again and my mother never recovered.

My father had quite a wonderful reputation in the communities where his presence was known. I am sure that I learned skills of navigating the world through his gift with words, both spoken and written – though not with his own children. He was articulate, warm, gentle, kind, and happy to help somebody that requested his wisdom. I never knew who he really was until I became an adult and we began to have real conversations. As the son of a woodcarver he inherited his father's dexterity and could do basic carpentry, as well as repair anything broken. He had the nickname "Mr. Fixit."

Had it not been for marrying my mother, I think he might have pursued an academic career. He was a budding socialist in the 1920s. However, to be welcomed by my mother's family he had to go into "business." He had experience working for a friend doing glass storefront repairs, so my grandparents and uncle financed the opening of Corona Plate Glass Company in 1925. (I have a cancelled company check for $75 that was used to pay for my parents' honeymoon.)

The glass company did well, and when I was a teenager it expanded into the manufacturing of aluminum and glass shower enclosures and patio doors. I loved working in the factory after school and during the summers. Machines sawing aluminum, large and small punch presses pounding and cutting notches and holes, sandblasting to etch designs on glass, assembling, shipping. It was an engineering wonder to my teenage eyes.

I had planned to gain some experience working elsewhere, but when I was nearing graduation at the Georgia Institute of Technology, an influential family member urged me to go to work for my father immediately after I graduate because "they really need you." I accepted the challenge. (I did not ask him, "How do you know they need me?" It just felt good to be needed.) As I would soon discover, his assertion was true, but unfortunately I was too late. One year later the company filed for bankruptcy. Devastated at the time, I can now look back and say it was a quintessential moment in my life, freeing me from family obligations to choose my own way in the world.

———————◇———————

My first wife and mother of my children, Dolores, discovered Montessori in 1965 because the woman who lived across the street worked in a Montessori school library. All prospective parents at the time were required to attend three meetings for their child to be considered for a Montessori school in Atlanta (there were only three). Mary Loew was the lecturer. She and I have known each other now for more than 50 years, and I will address our collaborative ventures later in this collection.

When my son, Warren, was four, I worried during a parent-teacher conference that he was "too sensitive." His teacher, Mary Frances replied, "The world needs sensitive people." Mary Frances suggested that I read Montessori's *Secret of Childhood* and, while thinking about the book on a drive home from work, I had to pull onto the freeway shoulder, stop my car, and pause, wondering how different my childhood would have been had I attended a Montessori school.

When Warren was six, he entered Martin Hall's Junior Class (that's what they called Montessori elementary in the early '70s). Martin was an ex-Jesuit monk and I always felt he had a mystical twinkle in his eyes. There were two other teachers, David Trower and Don Jenny. Don became a close personal friend. We talked about life and philosophy, framed pictures, and made furniture for his classroom. He is the one who asked "Why not now?" when I casually mentioned that I might be a Montessori teacher one day. David was a philosopher and introduced me to Teilhard de Chardin. Imagine, all three teachers for the older children were men. That really made an impact on me.

From age 25 through 32, while my children were attending the Montessori school, I was employed as a manufacturing engineer for a large military contractor. I took the job in the first place because I did not want to move to Fort Worth with my existing employer and because the salary was almost double what I had been making. I reasoned I could work for them because they were only building cargo aircraft, and that I would do so just until I could figure out something else to do. A value schism emerged. I loved the work and the security. I was climbing the corporate ladder, but inside, my heart was opposed to military spending and war of any kind. My tipping point occurred when they required all employees to sign a petition asking the national government to float a loan to stabilize the company debts. I was the only employee in 32,000 who refused. I was called to the division head's office to explain. I did not sign as requested – and, facing this in the mirror of self-reflection, resigned within a year. That first jump from well-paid known to unknown was really scary. But, I needed to do something that lifted my heart rather than filled my pockets. And in the end my heart was lifted and pockets were as deep as they needed to be.

As I began this writing process, I was perplexed by my inability to recall personal influences during my twenties: that is, from the time I graduated from university until the time that I was enveloped by the world of Montessori. Then I turned my attention, not to my chronological age, but to the years between 1962 and 1970. Those years made an indelible mark on my sense of justice, creating an ethical and moral framework for my entire life. There were three assassinations that colored the national and international landscape: President John Fitzgerald Kennedy, Martin Luther King, Jr., and Robert Kennedy. I was aghast that this could happen in the United States. During those eight years there was also massive civil rights unrest, the March on Washington, freedom riders, protesters against the war in Vietnam, and a wave of revolutionary thinkers called hippies, who turned everything inside out. Some literally dropped out, while others became strong embracers of right-action and love.

This turbulent decade wore its face every day in the media, and I was swept away by the encroachment of the march against liberty. Indeed, this intense period had me thinking deeply about right-action, core values, and how one would make a lasting impact on values so that children might grow up with a more inclusive notion of the world. It was natural for me to turn my attention to Montessori education as I witnessed first-hand my own children's experiences, and I understood the mindset and philosophical framework of many of the teachers.

During these tumultuous times one of my children's Montessori teachers suggested that I read Rollo May's *Man's Search for Himself*, which probes the personality to reveal the core of man's integration. That book opened a door for deeper searching that began in earnest a few years later when, at a certain moment, after a dead-end conversation with fellow workers, I walked towards my office through the perfect rows of engineers' desks and I realized there is no hope for humanity to change unless we change the system of education. Two years later I was headed to Bergamo, Italy to study the Montessori approach. Today I realize that the 1960s and my employment in the military industrial complex was the fodder that needed to be burned to create my new self.

While still employed as a manufacturing engineer, I rose in ranks to become a Department Manager. At 29, I was the youngest manager across the ranks. Outside of work, I was elected as vice president on the Montessori school's Board of Directors. I stood with the teachers when they requested salary increases. One of the other board members said that since teachers only worked until 3:00 pm, they could get jobs after school. He even offered a job to one of the teachers… to work in his laundry. The teachers caved-in despite my reminding them that they had the power: "No teachers, no school." It was not like there were any Montessori-trained teachers waiting in a queue for jobs.

I loved spending time at the school — seeing the children, and talking with the teachers. I started a parent group called "What's Next?" David Trower had given me Montessori's pamphlet on Erdkinder (her ideas on adolescence) and I wanted to help make it happen. That seed would eventually connect me to Maria Montessori's son Mario, grandson, Mario, Jr., and now great-grand-daughter, Carolina.

Just writing about all this is sending memories through my tissues and muscles — a strong interior excitement and anticipation — just like I had during the prelude to jumping from engineering to Montessori.

———————◇———————

I was first diagnosed with narcolepsy at age 21. Throughout the decade of my 20s I was taking 15-25 mg a day of amphetamines to keep awake. When I shifted to Italy for the Montessori teacher training, I brought a year's supply with me. One day, only a few weeks into the course, I forgot to take my medication. That stretched into two days, a week, a month, and I never had to take it again. I now understand how a physical manifestation can be imbedded in an emotional-psychological framework. I was not able to fully "awaken" until

I was doing something I was supposed to be doing. Thomas Berry calls it one's Great Work; Maria Montessori refers to it as one's Cosmic Task, and Joseph Campbell threads the process in his Hero's Journey. For me it was identifying with my soul's purpose. Surely Spirit was awakening me to what I was intended to do from the moment of birth – and the narcolepsy was Spirit's way of saying "Wake up to see the eyes of the world."

As a Montessori teacher I no longer felt like a fish trying to survive out of the water… and I could see why I had expressed that sensation during my childhood and early adult life.

I was uncomfortable
round the sarcasm
the arguing, and
that kind of humor.
I did not belong there.
No place to hide except
under the table.

School was never welcoming. It became a place for me to try to assert myself. "Philip talks back." They did not ask why; they just said, "Don't." I was that fish trying to feel safe and standing up for right-action, refusing to let teachers dress me down. I can still hear them say, "Who the hell do you think you are?"

Throughout childhood and early adult life I was thoroughly conditioned in and through the dominant paradigm where cause and effect ruled supreme. Engineering and management was the train I took to university and then into the world of work until I was 32 years old. The seeds planted and roots established throughout my early life sprung forth during that year, coming into awareness when a switch was turned on and a tunnel of light opened into view. It was when I said, "Yes" to "Why not now?"

It was the beginning of my Hero's Journey. I will explore this in depth later on, but for now I note that Joseph Campbell identifies three stages to the journey. The first, *separation*, occurs when the hero realizes there is something wrong with the picture of their life, the dominant paradigm, and listens instead to that still small voice within to follow one's bliss. *Initiation* is the transformational epoch in which new skills, new attitudes, and new learning takes place. Separation and initiation are followed by *return*, the time when the Hero takes the newly developed learning and shares it with others.

CHAPTER THREE:
LOVE AND ATTRACTION

Love comes through portals unknown
covered with the intimacy of
knowing-self, knowing-other, knowing-cosmos.
In the beginning there was Love,
manifesting as the cosmic web
from which we were born.
We are part of the interwoven fabric of Love
that permeates the cosmos
in a braided luminescence.
Unfolding
…throughout the Universe
…throughout Laniakea
…throughout the Milky Way
…throughout the Earth and among all beings
—sentient and non-sentient—
residents of this corner of evolution.

In 2008 Western science "discovered" the cosmic web, what Eastern mystics had known for millennia. They found that most of the Universe's matter was not contained in its billions of galaxies, but spread throughout the Universe in a web-like structure that exists in the spaces between galaxies. Then, in 2011, astronomers announced they "discovered proof of a vast filament of material that connects our Milky Way galaxy to nearby clusters of galaxies, which are similarly interconnected to the rest of the Universe."[11]

During my lifetime I have witnessed a steady stream of discoveries that scientifically demonstrate how the Earth and its inhabitants function as an interconnected web of being. Earth Systems Science shows us how the bio-geological cycles form a complex integrating network that sustains planetary balance. The cosmic web that has been identified "out there" resides "in here," on Earth – an echo of the understanding articulated by the crystal jewels in Indra's Net.

This web, or "filament-connecting nodes," not only appears in the celestial horizons, but also in our Milky Way and planetary system. We cannot "see" it on Earth; it is an *invisible thread* that connects all sentient and non-sentient beings. Identifying this invisible thread between himself and his prey, David James Duncan explains, "The forest Rishi's who set down the Rig Veda linked the atman, or 'soul' to the word sutr and called it the sutratman: 'soul-suture.' Early Coptic monks called it 'the indestructible connecting line.' Rumi identifies it as 'the cord of causation.'"[12] Whatever the name, it is the invisible evolutionary thread-connection that carries us forward from previous generations to the present and on into the future. I recognize it as a divine thread that connects everything in the cosmos.

As previously noted, Indra's Net symbolizes the Universe as an interpenetrating web of connections among all its entities, wherein every entity is both a manifestation of the whole and inseparable from the whole. Throughout time indigenous and native peoples have been viscerally connected to Earth and cosmos. For them there was no differentiation between the "out there" and "in here." All is one: a unity of creation's web.

In the beginning there was emptiness that was not quite as void as it was pregnant with possibility. Out of that empty but fertile reality was born everything we see and know – even the unseen and unknowable. The early cosmos was set into its evolution journey through its three basic tendencies that will be addressed in detail later in Chapter Ten: differentiation, autopoiesis, and communion. In my lecture at a 1985 Montessori international study con-ference, I identified three "cosmic laws" that were present from the beginning: interdependence, attraction, and unity. Several years later I would recognize interdependence as differentiation, attraction as autopoiesis, and unity as communion. I would recognize attraction as core to a developmental Universe. Cosmologist Brian Swimme explains, "We cannot fully explain why a proton is attracted to an electron . . . they are not being forced together by something called 'electromagnetic interaction.' Rather, it is by their very nature that they are drawn to each other."[13]

Might the force of attraction be the divine thread that permeates the Universe? Is it possible that the same force, which is responsible for coalescing particles, for keeping the entire cosmic web in balance through gravity, and for creating interdependent networks here on Earth, is nothing more than pure and essential love? What if the mysterious dark energy that scientists know is "out there" is merely an indication of cosmic love?

Perhaps love is the all-connecting manifestation of the Universe; it holds all matter in place; its very nature is celestial balancing; its very characteristic is cosmic harmony, permeating all things, boundless, deathless, infinite, and eternal. It is everywhere, and is the very heart of the heart of all that is.

Deep-seated, deep-rooted connections

Opening the portals to wider awareness

Embracing the cosmic dance of

Love.

Meaningful educating embraces this context by creating environments that bridge our connection to the universal. Teachers are learner-guides and learn-ers are teacher-guides. Process is confluent with content and content unfolds from a systemic perspective where one witnesses the interconnectedness and interdependencies that form the web of existence on Earth and in cosmos.

Everything enfolds from this worldview.

The science of how and why.

The mathematics of observation.
The art and beauty out of Earth's creativity.
The language arts to express and reflect upon the beauty.
And Love that gives birth to intimacy.

I was *attracted* to Montessori education. I was attracted when the time was right. When I look back now, I can see how people and events in my early life shaped that decision in the heart and mind of my 32-year-old self.

It was not until I was fully engaged in the process of becoming a Montessori teacher that I discovered and fully understood the congruence of Montessori ideas with my core values. Don Jenny said the word "consciousness" and piqued my curiosity. What was already occurring within my life to arouse this wonder? What was the source of my allurement to the word "consciousness"? I certainly was not exposed to that word or the ideas it contained in either my nuclear family or in the world of engineering. The recognition of Spirit, without the name to attach to it, did emerge with Ruth Gloria who showered me with cosmic love and opened my heart to see God in a profound way. I can see her now dancing and singing to gospel music; I went to her church and I met her God and I was open to the mystery, which I now see at least as a form of consciousness… an allurement that was dormant during my years as a scientist, engineer, and manager.

Actually, it was never totally dormant. Even though I worked in the military industrial complex, I had the only bumper sticker in the huge parking area for George McGovern presidency in 1972. I also had my passionate response to civil rights in the late '60s. So, I was in the mix but not of the mix. Still, narcolepsy disappeared when I went to Bergamo.

I rediscovered the allurement to consciousness in Montessori's own words:

That which we call love we have in our consciousness. It is the part of the universal energy that we feel consciously. But one may say that universal energy has nothing to do with humanity. Let us analyze it: it is an attraction, and what is attraction but a universal force. Let us consider the Universe. What keeps the stars where they are and makes them move along the fixed path they follow? Attraction. Why do bodies fall to the ground? By attraction. What is it that works among the atoms of matter so that they construct wholes? Attraction. If this attraction does not exist there would be chaos, nothing would be in existence. There would be no heaven and no stars without attraction. . . . Chemical affinity, which brings certain elements together, could not manifest itself without attraction. And attraction is love. . . the very essence of existence.[14]

A contemporary of Montessori's and another node in my personal cosmic web was the Jesuit theologian Pierre Teilhard de Chardin:

Driven by the forces of love, the fragments of the world seek each other so that the world may come into being. To perceive cosmic energy "at the fount" we must …. go down into the internal or radial zone of spiritual attractions. Love in all its subtleties is nothing more and nothing less than the… direct trace marked on my heart of the elements by the cyclical convergence of the Universe upon itself.[15]

These and more influences came in and through my life before I was 36 years old and set me on a path to discover a new lifelong orientation, expanding on those intersecting nodes in wider and wider spheres of exploration. Looking back now, I can see the titles and content of events that I principled over the years and notice how the context just kept moving further and wider — towards the exploration of education as a sacred and spiritual process that can contribute to inner and outer peace. I recall thinking about these things, but over the last few years these concepts have found a path to the written form. Much of this happened during an epic period in which the love of my life was passing through the veils between worlds.

The process of her decline forced me into looking deeply into who I was. How I moved from being "one that was not two" to "two that was one" and back to "one that was not two." I had no time while I was personally caretaking to explore anything that had to do with my own experience of her illness. Everything I did was focused on sustaining her needs and wants as well as a desire for her not to be humiliated by others. I had to struggle with the medical system as well as some of her children.

It was only after she was in full-time care that I began to explore the fullness of what happened and what presented itself to me for self-exploration and vision-carrier. I totally understand now that before her decline, I had some 20 years of a profound relationship with Marsha that brought me deep into understanding the meaning of love. Having a soulmate to co-create life with is an extraordinary journey. It truly was ecstatic in multiple domains. I will share more about this experience in the next chapter but suffice it to say for now that over the last few years I have been floating in a different energy field exploring the wonders of divine mystery.

In the beginning there was Love
manifesting as the cosmic web
from which we all originated.
We are part of the interwoven
fabric of Love that
permeates the cosmos
in an unfolding
braided luminescence.

CHAPTER FOUR:
SOULMATES

The soft embrace of lovers…
eyes locked in infinity.
Tenderness and light
Radiate

—

Eyes of a child
eyes of the world – wake up to see
you and me
in rhythm with
cosmic vibrations that
bring forth inner awareness.

We are the Universe reflecting upon itself.

What emerged at the beginning is here now. The energy and matter from the birth of the Universe – through time and differentiation – pass through cosmic nebulae, then stars, galaxies, and solar systems. Earth, and everything on, around and inside, is a further articulation of the presence at the beginning. Just like the crystal beads in Indra's Net, we are the Universe reflecting on itself… and understanding this changes everything.

Intellectually, I have known that we are the Universe reflecting on itself for many years. I connect to it viscerally when I am quiet and in a natural setting. At those moments I feel a deep connection with my surroundings, and my awareness of unity-within-diversity expands. I "see" as if for the first time, the absolute creativity that manifests in layers of intricate relationship: a creativity and creative expression that is a synonym for Love.

To experience this in one's lifetime is transformative. To experience that love with another person who shares the same vision is for me representative of soulmates or cosmic love. When Marsha Morgan and I finally embraced each other the way we each embraced the cosmos, it was after nearly 20 years of individually acknowledging the essence of Cosmic Education. At a certain point, there was nothing to do but to surrender to Love, despite the personal obstacles we both had to face and overcome in our lives apart from each other.

Marsha and I met on the plane of ideas with a sparkle in our eyes that evolved our previous understanding of Cosmic Love. With each other, we were able to feel "in here" what we had heretofore acknowledged as "out there." The notion that we could have that Love at the level of human love was a mystical fantasy for both of us, so when it presented itself, we were overwhelmed by Inspiration. Spirit was leading us both in one direction and neither of us could resist these cosmic forces.

Reflecting on our mutual life of co-creation that consumed a brief 20 years, I feel with absolute certainty that I had to experience the earthly cosmic love with Marsha in order to more deeply express the universal Cosmic Love. And the truth of that kind of cosmic love is… one day is miraculously enough to understand, but 25 years together feels like you've been cheated.

I felt so different in Marsha's company. We had similar sensitivities. She was spectacular at asking me the right question to draw out what I intrinsically knew but could not articulate. She knew that I knew, and I knew that she knew. I was in the company of someone who understood how my mind worked and would respond accordingly, allowing the total gift of my awareness to flower. I was in awe of Marsha's natural wisdom, wisdom born in the belly of right-action for the Earth and right-action in personal and group relationships. The windows to my own world were being cleared of dust.

> *Pulsing together*
> *creating bliss,*
> *planets and*
> *new stars.*
> *All one with Cosmos*
> *an external offer*
> *of spiritual dancing*
> *and cosmic awareness*
> *of not two, but one.*
> *Planet drum*
> *Gaian harmony*
> *melting into*
> *forever.*

By falling into bliss with the contexts of Cosmos and Gaia as primary, Marsha and I were able to live a life filled with right-action and love.

If there are lyrics that sum up our dance together, they are from Robert Hunter and Jerry Garcia's "Ripple."[16]

We were married in 1996 and for the next few years lived in Vermont six months of the year and Christchurch, New Zealand the other six months. This story is incomplete without me sharing the buildup to the wedding, especially with regards to Marsha's wonderful mother.

It was early Spring in Vermont and our thoughts turned to preparing for the first group of TIES graduate students. Marsha's 89-year-old mother, Kea, joined us in Grafton. She was a sweetheart, quiet, wise and with a twinkle of radiance in her eyes. As a graduate of Juilliard in the 1930s, she was a classical pianist for more than 60 years teaching children and adults as well as playing piano and organ at church every Sunday. Kea and I were very good friends. She loved reading my Uncle Bill's handwritten letters. He was 100 years and still going strong.

Marsha and I were eating lunch at a café in Brattleboro. It was quint-essential Vermont, complete with a stream in the back. The scene, the music, the atmosphere was just perfect. The question rolled off my lips like ripples in still water. "What would Kea say if you got married again?" Marsha queried back, "Do you have anyone in mind?" We laughed and cried while listening in the background to Billie Holiday singing "Moonlight in Vermont." Oh, how many times we peered into the winter nights to see moon glow reflecting off the birch trees casting shadows on the white blanket of snow below. However beautiful winter, we chose the summer solstice – June 21 – to celebrate our wedding… "in ripple time"… as Marsha would name it.

After Marsha went through the veil between worlds, I found a tiny blue vase in her desk drawer. Inside was a small strip of paper with these words written on both sides:

In that space between dreaming and awakening
Remember who you are & that you are Love(d)

In Brian Swimme's video series, *Powers of the Universe*,[17] he identifies 11 pow-ers that are imbedded in how the Universe responds to novelty: seamlessness, centration, allurement, emergence, homeostasis, cataclysm, synergy, trans-mutation, transformation, interrelatedness, and radiance. In each of the 11 videos he explains how these themes can be explored through the lens of our own lives. Marsha and I lived in all these domains. It wasn't always easy, but in the tension creative emergence appeared.

In the documentary about his life, *Monte Grande*,[18] Chilean biologist, philosopher, and neuroscientist Francesco Varela is asked, "What is so special about your relationship with Amy Cohen?" He responds, "I can fit all of me into it." Marsha and I viewed this inspiring film many times over the years, but it was only recently that I realized the primal paradox built within Varela's statement about wholeness, individuality, and creativity. Finally, I was able to come to grips with the personal and professional primal paradox with Marsha.

According to system scientists, Fritjof Capra and Pier Luigi Luisi, "The double role of living systems as parts and wholes requires the interplay of two opposite tendencies: an integrative tendency to function as part of a larger whole, and a self-assertive, or self-organizing tendency to preserve individual autonomy."[19] The primal paradox revealed in my relationship with Marsha is a derivative of this living systems' perspective. It addresses the autonomy and relationship aspects of autopoietic processes (see Chapter Ten).

When I proposed to take our vision out into the world, her typical response was "I just want a simple life, planting a garden and being with children." She was very protective of her ideas and often kept them secret from me until they were fully formed. I would be ecstatic about her creativity and insight and ready to apply them to our work. She would be reluctant.

My own view was that ideas were free, born to be shared – especially those that might be a catalyst for others along their journey. My common response to these differences with Marsha was not to push my agenda. Why? Because I wanted to avoid potential conflict. Herein lay the crux of our primal paradox: the tension between one's drive to be an individual and the drive to collaborate with others. In order to preserve what we experienced as heart-connected, twin-soul love, I chose to sacrifice some of my ethos.

Obviously we each brought our personal history/cosmic thread into the relationship and that conditioning prevented us from seeing what we could not see. As a result, I lost some of my personal creative expression, which resurfaced when Marsha went into full-time care in 2014 and then passed away in 2017. The creative tension in our work together bore amazing fruits, and I have no regrets for what might have been because we had a glorious life together. Now, however, the Universe is allowing me to be joyfully reacquainted with my creating self, a self that needed those earlier collaborative stepping-stones to find the new path before me.

CHAPTER FIVE:
LEADERSHIP AS INSPIRATION

All over nature, throughout the Gaian system, right under our noses,
so to speak, and all around us, we find the clues to making our own human
affairs more organic and ethical.
Elisabet Sahtouris [20]

If I am right the whole of our thinking of what we are and the way
other people are has to be restructured. The most important task today
is to learn to think in a new way.
Gregory Bateson [21]

There is a spark, a thread, a filament that permeates time and space connecting us to the still small voice within. When that connection results in inspiration for right-action, inner leadership emerges. Sometimes others witness this quality and align themselves with the same values and shared leadership emerges. Throughout my life, led by Inspiration, I have found myself standing in my truth, standing up for Truth, which has placed me in leadership positions. In my youth I had no idea how to manage that territory and often sabotaged myself. At a certain moment in time I understood how shared leadership – one that empowers others in the process – reflects and mirrors the way I worked with children in my Montessori class. That was certainly true with GATE and TIES.

"And the little child shall lead them," quietly whispered from the other side of the room by Ruth Gloria while I am in a confrontation with my parents. Lead what? Lead whom? My takeaway was that Ruth was protecting me.

When I was 12 years old and new to the neighborhood, a crew of play-mates knocked on my front door and announced that I was kicked out of the "Daredevils." Devastated, I hold back the tears. My crime? I left a hammer in our tree house. I am punished, sacked for two weeks. What kind of leadership is that? Might my friends' actions be a derivative of a cultural imperative toward reward and punishment, the backbone of our educational system?

As a teenager I was elected president of a social club. Why was I chosen? Why did I care to be chosen? I remember having an ability to organize ideas and to see contexts. As long as the New York Yankees won the World Series, truth and right-action were my guideposts. I honestly believed that truth and right-action *was* the New York Yankees.

During my university years, I was part of a fraternity leadership coup. The other group believed that ends justify means, while "my" side thought that right-action should determine means. My side won and I was elected the new president, with a lot of enemies. I did not realize it at the time, but winning has a shadow side. I don't believe there must always be winners and losers, but it often seems to play out that way.

I was not placed in a leadership role when I went to work for my father after graduating from university. However, everyone in the factory knew that it was only a matter of time. I would never be accepted as one of the men. I felt an element of distrust, which might have been justified. Why? As I said earlier, even before I finished my bachelor's degree, a trusted family member pulled me aside and *told* me that I must go to work for my father after graduation from Georgia Tech, declaring, "You are the only one who can save the business."

That was a pretty heavy message to give a 21-year-old. After all, my older brother had been working for my dad for nearly 15 years. What did Sy see in me that I did not see? I was totally amazed by his confidence and then took on that burden of "saving the business." After all, *I am a manufacturing engineer, and I can see how to organize things.* I never told anybody that sentiment, but it must've been written all over my face.

My father's business went bankrupt one year after I started working for him. Although devastated at the time, I count that devastation as one of the most significant gifts in my life. I was free. I escaped from New York. I no longer *belonged* in New York, and certainly not in any proximity to my extended family. Married just over a year, my first wife, Dolores, and I packed our belongings and headed back to Atlanta, her birthplace, and where I had attended Georgia Tech. It was a greener and gentler place to live. In the midst of our getting ready to leave New York, the world stood still on November 22, 1963, when President John F. Kennedy was assassinated. I was a strong admirer of his principles and captivated by his charisma. A living hero, he was taken down in the prime of his life. Like many of the youth in America, Kennedy represented a fresh new look in politics; his charisma was contagious with remarks like, "Tolerance implies no lack of commitment to one's own beliefs. Rather it condemns the oppression or persecution of others," or "War will exist until that distant day when the conscientious objector enjoys the same reputation and prestige that the warrior does today." The dream that was lost with his death is still waiting in the wings.

I lived in Atlanta for a short while. My dad's business was sold in bankruptcy to a company in Tuscaloosa, Alabama. Despite my youth and inexperience, they hired me to run the small plant. Tuscaloosa was way off my radar and I could not bear living in a place where my beliefs and values were not in alignment with the dominant Southern way of life at that time. We soon returned to Atlanta where I gained employment with a manufacturer of aluminum building products. My standout memory was when I created a method for employee evaluation that used a sliding scale rather than checkboxes. It was rather revolutionary! Shortly thereafter I was flown to Chicago to tour the home office and factory and to have dinner at the residence of the company president. At dinner I was offered the position as plant manager for their branch in Fort Worth, Texas. I was 25.

I still wonder what they observed in me. Enthusiasm? Positive work ethic? Amicability? How is it that I was offered a leadership position without having ever experienced a leadership role? What an opportunity!

Or was it?

Despite not wanting to move from Atlanta where my cultural and spiritual roots were in formation, I flew to Fort Worth to check things out. On a lark, the day before the trip, I applied for a manufacturing engineering position at Lockheed-Georgia. Rationalizing that the plant to which I applied was only building military cargo planes, not the planes that were dropping bombs, I was ready to take the job – just until I found something else – as it represented a serious increase in income over the Fort Worth opportunity. Lockheed hired me.

I took my place at a desk amongst a sea of desks. I was shocked to see people in salaried positions watching the clock. Starting and stopping to the sound of a whistle took me by surprise. One day I was finishing some work and stayed beyond quitting time. A coworker said, "You'll get over that." I never did. Within a year I was working in a much smaller office, reporting directly to George Reddein, head of one of the manufacturing divisions. A year after that I was promoted to a department manager. At age 28 I was the youngest manager among 33,000 employees. Reddein told me, "In a crowd of people there is always one head above the rest, and you are that one." I remember thinking "How did this happen?" All the other men that had become managers were required to go to "management training," and never having been invited to do so, I thought I was not good enough.

As a department manager, I discovered how to listen and help people take ownership for their responsibilities. I promoted workers to supervisory positions even when advised that they were not worth the risk. The work engaged all of my skills and initiative. I loved finding solutions to problems. Embracing the challenges of leadership made it easier to overlook the fact that I was working for a military contractor. One success led to another and I could see my skills expanding. I learned how the system worked, and I got results. I could see myself climbing the corporate ladder. Life was quite wonderful. I had a financially rewarding job, and at home, Dolores and I were parenting a son and daughter. I even forgot that Lockheed was supposed to be a temporary job.

As I mentioned earlier, a day came when I had to "face the music" that to me was off-key. My superiors came to me at the height of the Vietnam conflict and said, "All employees are signing this petition to ask the US government to guarantee a federal loan so that the company can remain financially solvent. Why haven't you signed?" Within a year after refusing to sign that petition, I quit. The dissonance between the values of the organization and my own psychological shifts – *awakening* through an exploration of philosophy and psychology – had become intolerant. What I did not realize at the time, was that the Montessori world was also opening up inside my heart. That next step was six months down the road.

I had no idea what was next. My father introduced me to one of his colleagues who had just begun manufacturing small steam generators that convert home showers into steam rooms. I saw the product in action and I was totally convinced... for less than six months.

When I was nine, Divine Spirit sent me an angel in the form of Ruth Gloria, who befriended me during my adolescent years. Now Spirit stepped in again and sent Don Jenny, who, as I mentioned earlier, was a Montessori teacher at the school where my children were enrolled. We became good friends and had long dialogues about life. I recall helping him make the *Time Line of Life*, a Montessori lesson for elementary-aged children that depicts the evolution of life on Earth. It ended with the Cenozoic Age. "I wonder what comes next?" I asked. He replied, "Perhaps the Age of Consciousness." At the time I was reading Pierre Teilhard de Chardin's *Phenomenon of Man*, which helped me understand the journey of consciousness. I could not believe the synchronicity.

Six weeks after Don Jenny's "Why not now?" question, Spirit swung into motion for me to become a Montessori teacher. My wife, along with 8-year-old Warren and 4-year-old, Sharon, were aboard Icelandic Airlines headed for a final destination of Bergamo, Italy, where Dolores and I would take the year-long teacher training course at Centro Internazionale di Studi Montessoriani, while our children went to Scuola Montessori.

Bergamo was a most transformative experience. For the first time in my life I no longer felt that I was a fish out of water; I was in the water learning to swim with other fish. The course of study, like all Montessori training, was not given in a Montessori way. It did not provide contextualized meaning for the adult learner. By the end of the year I had to make sense of it all. I constructed a large flow chart, bar-graphing the seven curriculum areas and the distribution of lessons over the six elementary years. It was relational so one could integrate the "subject" areas. I also created a key to the charts that listed each lesson within each bar sequence. I shared this exploration with the director of training, Eleonora Honegger, and she requested a copy. Much to my surprise when I went for my final oral exam, the external examiners were using my chart and outline as their reference.

Part way through the year I made a formal request to observe Scuola Montessori's program for children over the age of 12. My motivation took root several years earlier when, as a parent, I asked one of the teachers, "What happens in Montessori after 12 years of age?" He gave me a booklet that contained two Maria Montessori lectures from the 1930s. It was titled, *The Erdkinder and the Function of the University*. It got my attention. Since the booklet was no longer in print I made photocopies and invited other interested parents to a series of meetings to explore the ideas. Now that I was in Bergamo, I wanted to see what they were doing.

After a short visit I understood their reluctance to open the doors to visitors, as the program basically had nothing to do with Montessori's vision. This thread, this exploration of Montessori adolescent education, would grow and blossom in my work for the next 15 years. My interest in this age group led to me getting to know both Maria Montessori's son, Mario Montessori, and her grandson, Mario Montessori, Jr. I began to implement a plan for adolescence at my school, and then Life intervened. It seems Inspiration had another unexplored path that I was destined to develop: a graduate school program based on Montessori principles and philosophy.

Where did this passion about adolescence take root? Why was I so motivated? Perhaps it was a response to heal my own adolescent journey. Perhaps I recognized that the entire Montessori vision for education from birth through university could plant seeds for a new human and a new Earth community. Perhaps both.

When we returned to the United States from Italy, I was appointed the Montessori school's administrator and taught part time. I only wanted to teach, but I was the one most qualified to take the position of Administrator. The school was a cooperative with all 12 teachers having a voice in decision-making. That process was exhausting with meetings going late into the evening and disrupting our lives. It affected the classroom the next day and caused angst for those of us with children who needed attention in the evenings. A clear division amongst the faculty emerged. Along with four other teachers representing one of the school's three locations, I proposed that we go our own way. The five of us had become good friends and shared a common spiritual orientation. The predominantly black parent body from our location supported us, as they felt disempowered by the all-white "other side of the city" management.

Presented with this option, the rest of the teachers turned us down. We were resolute and went ahead with plans to create our own school. Identified as the "ringleader" I was fired midyear, charged with "mutinying covertly." It was heartbreaking to leave the children without being allowed to say goodbye. The entire incident forced me into an emotional maelstrom. This was a resurrection of my mother's "you'll get yours," and "getting caught."

There was one rather humorous incident during this emotional minefield. Both sides were meeting with the Episcopalian minister of the church that housed our location. He wanted to know what was going on. He actually said, "One day I walked out of the office and Moses was leading his people away." That remark provided an inner smile. I experienced it as a metaphor for right-action leadership. "Jumping" for me has persistently marked shifting paradigms and assuming leadership.

As my son, Warren, inched his way towards adolescence I became more deeply involved with Montessori's ideas for this age. *Erdkinder*, translated from German as "earth-children," was the word Maria Montessori used to describe a rural, farm-based, learning environment for early adolescents. She believed young people needed a visceral experience of working the land while comprehending the origins of exchange and economics, and where "academics" were integrated with real life experience. This, according to Montessori, would make them better capable of serving humanity. Thirty years later I would re-conceptualize her ideas into an ecological and sustainable living framework in an urban environment. And just recently I became acutely aware that her ideas on adolescence were expressed in 1937 and did not include any reflections of how her worldview shifted during her years in India (1939-1946).

Montessori's vision for adolescents came alive for me in an article I wrote titled "A School for My Children."[22] Soon after its publication, I helped form an Erdkinder study group. My close colleague, Mary Loew, along with a few other Montessori teachers and parents, began meeting regularly. When Mary mentioned to me that the Montessori teacher trainers from around the world were gathering in close-by Helen, Georgia for their annual meeting, we took the opportunity to invite Betty Stephenson and Abs Joosten, two well-known Montessori teacher trainers, to one of our gatherings. The audio recordings of that meeting were transcribed, edited, and sent to a number of notable Montessorians in Europe, including Mario Montessori and Mario Montessori, Jr.

A few months later I received an envelope from Holland containing a 13-page letter from Mario Montessori, Jr. At the time he was an advisor to the Association Montessori Internationale (AMI). Maria Montessori founded AMI in 1929 and with her death in 1952, her son, Mario, Sr. became its global leader. In addition to his voluntary position with AMI, Mario Montessori, Jr. was a practicing psychoanalyst and vice president of the International Psychoanalytic

Association. He had recently published the book, *Education for Human Development*, which included an impressive forward by Buckminster Fuller.

That written response from Mario, Jr. became a seminal document for the Montessori movement. Years later, after we had been friends for a long time, he told me his passion for the education of adolescence had its roots at the feet of his grandmother's observations of him and other grandchildren during 1930s family summer holidays on a farm in Germany. We continued to correspond until he died 15 years after our first meeting. I stayed with him at his summer home in the north of Holland and in the late '80s he served on my doctoral committee.

Back in 1978, a year after Mario, Jr. and I began corresponding, I was invited to the Montessori Institute of Atlanta because Mario, Sr. was visiting and wanted to meet me. I assumed his son told him to "check me out." I must have passed the test because over the ensuing years I became quite close to both Mario Jr. and Sr.

Mary Loew and I asked for Mario, Sr.'s. approval to convene *Adolescence: An Exploration,* an AMI International Study Conference in Atlanta. We invited him to attend, but at age 81 and in fragile health, he declined. Eventually he changed his mind and came to Atlanta because, in his own words, "I wanted to feel for the last time the perfume of the movement moving on to the adolescent work after my death." During the conference, Mary and I recorded a video interview with Mario, Sr.[23] It was his last public appearance.

After the conference my son and I went to Europe for his 16th birthday, spending the first week in Holland. Upon landing in Amsterdam, we were retrieved by Mario, Sr. and his wife, Ada, who drove us to the north of Holland where we met Mario, Jr. at his summer home. During the drive Mario told me about how the Nazis had proclaimed that the war (World War II) would "be the end of Montessori in Europe."

Later that year I received a copy of a letter Mario, Jr. sent on my behalf to the teacher training nomination committee. Reading that recommendation 35 years later, I realize it's prophetic nature. Mario, Jr. had extraordinary insights into who I was, insights that I did not understand for a long time. Here is the main portion of that letter with the prophetic line in italics:

> Phil Gang and I have been in touch with each other through his work concerning the Erdkinder project, about which he consulted me. Since that first contact we have met several times. Although ours has been mainly a working relationship based on discussions related to Montessori education, a more personal note soon entered into it, growing – at least as far as my own feelings are concerned – into a friendship.
>
> I find him a very fine person indeed, intelligent, warm, sensitive and modest, but with the courage of his convictions, which gives a special kind of strength to his character, quite different from that found in ambitious people pursuing personal aims.
>
> He is a dedicated person. Enterprising; with a realistic outlook; not giving up easily but *recognizing the limitations presented by a given situation and abiding by them until a new opportunity offers itself to bring whatever he is doing a step further.*
>
> I find him creative and differentiated in his thinking as well as emotionally, and above all sensible. Also sincere in his motivation. A devoted Montessorian, who has understood the values of what our movement has to offer and who is prepared to participate in it even more actively than he has done to date. We are badly in need of young persons with this attitude toward our work.

That italicized line is exactly what happened eight years later, when I left the organized Montessori community in another juncture of Campbell's Hero's Journey.

In 1982, Mario, Sr. passed away, and I started the apprenticeship to become a Montessori teacher trainer. The next summer I attended a meeting for Montessori teacher trainers near Mexico City. Maria Montessori's youngest granddaughter, Renilde, sat beside me during a bus excursion to a rural community. We had a delightful conversation and struck up a dialogue about her grandmother's nomination for the Nobel Peace Prize. The AMI had already convened two international congresses on the subject of peace and education. Now, with the Cold War in a mad march towards annihilation, I thought the time was ripe to do this again. She agreed. With her backing, Mary Loew and I wrote to Ada Montessori, who had become the movement's leader. She concurred, and in 1985, Atlanta hosted the *AMI International Study Conference: Education and Peace.*

My keynote address took the pre-computer form of a multi-media presentation: *The Cosmology of Peace.* I was gobsmacked by the response. Invitations came to take that presentation, along with elements from the conference, on the road the following year to four additional locations in the United States, eventually offering it in Italy, New Zealand, and Australia. The Italy invitation came from Antonietta Paolini, who was well into her 80s and was not only trained in 1930 by Maria Montessori, but a very close friend of the family. Over the next few years I also gave similar presentations in France, Sweden, Norway, Finland, Mexico, Brazil, Canada, Venezuela, and even in the Soviet Union.

One year later, I withdrew from the Montessori Training of Trainer's Program because of the incongruence between the delivery of the method and the expectations for teachers in the classroom. For me the process of preparing teachers had to emulate the process expectations of those teachers in their classrooms. There had to be a more collaborative, integrating process. I wanted to research how this might be accomplished. My 1985 *Cosmology of Peace* lecture became one of the roots of this inquiry. It had planted a seed that continued to grow. It was the perfect opportunity for me to further my education so I enrolled in a self-directed doctoral program through The Union Institute and University. My PhD journey was quite special, not only for the self-creative process, but also because my paths crossed with another person who changed the way I approached life. Donald Klein was my mentor and guide throughout my studies. He was to me an intellectual mystic, simultaneously supportive and always there to ask the right question. Above all else, he lived the philosophy of right-action. He was the first person who recognized my integration of engineer-scientist with intellectual-humanitarian. After I graduated and had created TIES, he wrote the following:

May the moon
Of your energy
Shine through
The trees
Of possibility
May it bathe
Your world
In success
To the roots
Of your
Intentions
May it create
TIES
That help
To empower
A knowing
World
At Peace.

My dissertation was titled, *The Emerging Paradigm and Secondary Education*, later published as my first book, *Rethinking Education*. This work explores the basic tenets of macro and micro physics and applies those organizing principles to education and learning. Throughout the '70s and '80s, I was captivated by revelations in cosmology as well as the "new" particle physics. These contexts took center stage along with the cosmology of peace for conceptualizing how to situate education.

The Cosmology of Peace presentation continued to live on through my dissertation and the TIES work. It found its way into additional worldwide presentations as part of my role in the Global Alliance for Transforming Education (GATE).

A key figure in the spread of GATE's ideas was Robert Muller, Assistant Secretary-General of the United Nations. I first met Muller at the UN when I invited him to participate in the Education and Peace conference. During that initial meeting he gave me a prerelease copy of Brian Swimme's first book, *The Universe is a Green Dragon*.[24] Excerpts from that book found their way directly into my keynote address as they provided a seamless context for Montessori's Cosmic Education. Eventually Brian and I crossed paths, and we have stayed connected. Muller was the consummate networker, even writing a poem, printed on a postcard, titled, "Decide to Network."

> *Decide to network,*
> *In a world of big powers, media, and monopolies*
> *But of six billion individuals*
> *Networking is the new freedom*
> *the new democracy*
> *a new form of happiness.*

Many of my experiences during the 1980s would not have unfolded had I not decided to leave the Montessori school I started in 1978. After leading the "revolution" and making the necessary decisions to create Southwest Montessori, I just wanted to teach and not have any administrative responsibilities. A Montessori colleague and founder of another school in Atlanta died during the 1979-1980 academic year. The children were in a state of shock and had no teacher. I volunteered to help a few afternoons a week. I enjoyed "just being a teacher," so when the administrative secretary asked me if I would consider working full-time the following year, there was a moment of silence before I jumped into this opportunity.

At last, no administrative responsibility. I could just teach. That first group of children has forever been in my heart: Greg, Antoinette, Michelle, Janet, Kristen, Sharon, Joy, Norman, and Georgie. I am still in touch some of them 40 years later.

During that first year I was often approached for administrative guidance. The school decided to open another location 30 minutes closer to my home. We were all amazed by the success of this initiative. When I went to work for the school in 1980, there were 60 students. I became head of Northwoods Montessori School and moved out of the classroom at about the same time we initiated a secondary program. When I left in 1987, I had helped grow the school to an enrollment of 225.

I resigned from Northwoods for a number of reasons. No longer challenged by the work and disappointed with Montessori organizations, which included schools, I wanted to strike a chord for a new, integrating voice that would advocate not just for Montessori ways but also for educating along the entire holistic spectrum.

Until I moved to New Zealand, my experience in Montessori schools always fell short of expectations. I wanted to see Montessori principles applied to school structure and relationships. I thought there could be adult learning communities, just like the ones we created for children. This is a challenging objective because even if the adults embrace the Montessori vision, many of them do not explore their own psychological world. At the root of that exploration is insight into how conditioning drops one into unexplored assumptions. Freeing ourselves from conditioning is primary for creating authentic communities. In New Zealand I found just that school: Nova Montessori. It was founded by Marsha Morgan and her colleague Pauline Matsis. I believe it accomplished that integrity because of its intent to not only follow Montessori guidelines, but also to embrace Jiddu Krishnamurti's approach to inquiry.

Krishnamurti came into my lens when my renegade brother-in-law came home for a visit during the mid '70s. Jerry had left Atlanta in a cloud of dust many years earlier. Talk about someone who did not fit into the dominant paradigm, he had a creative mind in a dysfunctional family where he was misunderstood, rejected and physically abused. Jerry took out an LP and told me to listen carefully to every word. It was an audio recording of a talk given by Krishnamurti and marked the first time I heard the words "conditioned mind." I was captivated by his words and secured my first Krishnamurti book, *Think on These Things*. In time, I would discover Krishnamurti's ideas on dialogue and how they influenced David Bohm. The principles of dialogue were significant in Marsha's and my collaborative work and have been a main thread in our M.Ed. programs.

———————◇———————

I met Ron Miller while attending an Association for Humanistic Psychology (AHP) conference at Curry College in 1986. My involvement with AHP was another door-opening experience as I was invited to join a delegation of "citizen diplomats" who journeyed to the Soviet Union in October, 1987. I felt like a pioneer crossing new territory, going into the unknown. Before we left Helsinki, bound for our first stop, in Leningrad, the delegation came together to hear from seasoned Soviet visitors about protocols "behind the iron curtain." I remember thinking "What in the world am I doing?" We visited Soviet schools in Leningrad (now St. Petersburg), Moscow, and Tbilisi (now Republic of Georgia). That was my first of five trips as part of AHP's Global Education Project. During the second visit, underneath a large painting of Russian revolutionary Vladimir Lenin, I gave a lecture about Montessori education to the Soviet Academy of Arts and Sciences.

Another time I traveled on my own – arriving in Moscow and transferring to Aeroflot for an overnight flight to Irkutsk, Siberia. The flight was horrifying with only overhead nets to hold luggage. I couldn't move my 6'2" frame in those tiny seats. Luckily I convinced (without words) a young boy, who had a seat missing in front of him, to trade with me in exchange for some apples I brought with me from Sweden. The kind of fruit I offered, which wasn't available in the Soviet Union, lit up his eyes. In addition to presenting my ideas to Soviet ecological educators, I participated in a birch sauna followed by a dive into Lake Baikal, which was undergoing ecological rehabilitation.

After the 1986 AHP gathering, Ron Miller visited my school in Atlanta where we talked about his new project – the creation of a journal that focused on holistic education. In 1988 one of my articles was published in the first issue of the *Holistic Education Review*. Ron and I kept in contact and in early 1989 I rang him to suggest that we convene a gathering of holistic educators that would represent the full spectrum of individuals and groups holding a slice of the holistic pie – just to see what might emerge. I thought, "Why not work together to make an even stronger statement?"

Six months later, Ron said, "You know that holistic gathering you suggested, I think it is time." In late 1989 we formed a steering committee and eight of us from across the US gathered at the Center for New Beginnings just north of Atlanta. We designed an event to be held in Chicago the following summer, inviting 80 individuals to "create a common vision for holistic education."

I extended an invitation to Robert Muller to open the conference. By then he was the Chancellor for the UN University for Peace in Costa Rica. He was unable to attend but sent his colleague Abelardo Brenes with the charge that "You must issue a statement after the event that will get people's attention." We took his advice and published the *1990 Chicago Statement on Education* (see Appendix I), which set the stage for the creation of GATE. The following year GATE adopted the document *"Education 2000: A Holistic Perspective"* (see Appendix II).

GATE received some funding and I was appointed executive director. As an advocate of its ten core principles, I traveled throughout the world sharing the vision. The document was translated into French, Spanish, Italian, Japanese, Portuguese, and Polish. Wherever I went, people in the audience would always ask where they might be able to learn to teach according to these principles. This interest and desire planted the seed for the development of the TIES M.Ed. programs.

Edward T. Clark was a member of the GATE steering committee and a well-known holistic education systems thinker. Upon hearing his approach to "mapping" contextual relationships in an ecosystem, I knew this had to be incorporated into any teacher preparation program that I created. Marsha Morgan, by then a long-time friend, was also interested in ecological relationships, so I invited her to hear Clark's presentation at a Goddard College

GATE gathering in Vermont. Marsha built on Clark's ideas over the next 20 years developing her own process called "Natural Mapping by Gaian Design," which is addressed in Chapter Seven.

The years between 1988 and 1996 brought many opportunities for me to see branches of possibility proliferate on the tree of my life:

- Leaving the community of organized Montessori organizations
- Founding The Institute for Educational Studies (TIES)
- Traveling as a citizen diplomat to the Soviet Union on several occasions
- Developing the teaching material, *Our Planet, Our Home*
- Traveling throughout North and South America, Europe, the Far East, and South Pacific: Sharing the GATE Vision and giving seminars on *Transforming Education: A Holistic Approach.*
- Falling into twin-soul love with Marsha
- Creating a Montessori course for teachers – first in Oslo and then in Vancouver, where Marsha and I practiced congruence between how we worked with adults and how we expected Montessori adults to be with children
- Leaving Atlanta after 35 years, as well as my marriage of 30 years
- Accepting a faculty position at the California Institute of Integral Studies (CIIS) in the School for Transformative Learning – one of the first online doctoral programs
- Founding the TIES M.Ed. program in Integrative Learning

The circumstances that opened the doorways to leadership positions were, for me, catalyzed by right-action, following Truth, and guided by those, listening to my inner voice.

CHAPTER SIX:
THE GREAT RIVER

The cosmic river...
whose heart flows with the river of cosmic kindness.
whose soul flows with the river of cosmic gladness.
whose goal flows with the river of cosmic oneness.
Sri Chinmoy [25]

This chapter has been writing itself since the day I was born. The title comes from a lecture of the same name from my Montessori six to twelve studies in 1973. It is an introductory fable to the study of the human body told to children between the ages of 9 and 12. The great river is a metaphor for the circulatory system that courses through each human enabling all organisms in the body to carry out their functions. However, the story is not merely about the human body. Like many Montessori lessons it leads to an understanding of greater cosmic work, the work that manifests throughout creation where an entity is seemingly concerned with its own needs but in meeting those, contributes to the greater whole. Montessori goes on to compare the human circulatory system to the infinite network of exchanges on Earth that unites the world.

Montessori uses the word "cosmic" to describe a force that manifests throughout creation, one that establishes an intricate web of connections and interdependencies, just like the crystal beads in Indra's Net. In a London lecture (1935) she explains, "The child with his simplicity of action, works in harmony with the cosmos. We (adults) must enter into harmony and take up that which is of central importance: our own cosmic work . . ."[26] Later in *To Educate the Human Potential* (1948) she writes, ". . . the fundamental principle in education is the correlation of all subjects, and their centralization in the cosmic plan."[27]

Montessori's ideas on Cosmic Education will be examined in Chapter Nine: "Giving Back Montessori to Montessori."

For many years I have been exploring my life as a river of influences and confluences – people and events – that are tributaries, flowing into the river of my conscious awareness. It has been a search for deeper understanding and insight into my own life, while exploring the influences that were catalysts for Inspiration.

Years after my Montessori studies and my work with children, I was leading a series of seminars, *Transforming Education, Transforming Ourselves.* I found the following "notes to the teacher" from the *The Great River* lesson where Montessori says, "In order to teach/direct other people it is necessary to first transform ourselves for it is not possible to be a teacher without transforming oneself."[28]

If one is exploring transformation of self, one needs to know what is being transformed. I asked seminar participants to "draw the river of their lives" highlighting people and events that were instrumental in their journey. As the participants drew their images, I joined the activity and in that moment became emotionally connected to the process. Without conscious reflection two keynotes emerged – Ruth Gloria's influence and the discovery of Montessori. A few years later when I repeated the activity, I added a third keynote that I labeled "cosmic love" – the Marsha tributary.

I began thinking about the Great River on a cosmic scale. Might that river be a metaphor for the flow of awareness-consciousness throughout the universe? Might the river represent consciousness itself – the Source, the Ground that is the undifferentiated unity of all that is? It is challenging to find the words to describe the awareness that has emerged as I witness all those events that have flowed through my river. It is as if there is a divine manifestation or thread of inspiration for right-action that I can observe through my life-experience river of awareness-consciousness.

My intuition, combined with an exploration of Montessori's years in India (see Chapter Nine), leads me to the conclusion that Divine wisdom flowed through Maria Montessori's personal Great River. She did not set out with an intention to develop a system of education that was rooted in Spirit. Her objective was to discover what experiences are necessary to liberate childhood – and thus adults – to reach their potential. In doing so, her vision embraced the notion that transformed consciousness would be the catalyst for the emergence of a *new human* ". . . who will not be the victim of events, but will have the clarity of vision to direct and shape the future of human society."[29]

Consciousness is the spark of awareness that connects each of us to the universal. It is the thread that binds the knower with the known in such a way that Truth itself may become visible. Right-action is a cosmic consequence of understanding that Truth. Maria Montessori observes, ". . . there is a slow development of consciousness that reveals itself as it realizes itself."[30] Montessori refers to the notion that one's consciousness expands as opportunities arrive to become aware of oneself. And that awareness is the journey of the self toward the Self.

Her approach to child development is renowned for helping children bring to consciousness what has been stored in the preconscious or subconscious. This process of indirect preparations essentially results in phrases like, "I taught myself," inferring a liberation of sorts. She was strongly influenced by the writings of British biologist, Julian Huxley, who claimed that, "Humans are that part of reality in which and through which the cosmic process has become conscious and has begun to comprehend itself." [31]

Throughout my life I have been searching for the seeds of such cosmic processes. What is underneath the underneath? The question, "Why?" was more than a child's rhetorical response. It seems I was on a quest for context, understanding how everything fits. Why is biology separate from geography? Why is chemistry separate from physics? Why world history? Why American history? Why not Earth history or Universe history? Isn't everything a derivative of the Universe? Shouldn't the Universe story be primary? Responses to these kinds of questions sat on a shelf for years and then slowly, as I began to go deeper into my personal journey and found Montessori education, I eventually experienced the pulse of *all is one*.

Quoting U Thant, the third Secretary-General of the United Nations, Robert Muller offered one of the most significant responses to that pulse:

> Spirituality is a state of connectedness to life. It is an experience of being, belonging and caring. It is sensitivity and compassion, joy and hope. It is the harmony between the innermost life and the outer life, or the life of the world and the life of the universe. It is the supreme comprehension of life in time and space, the tuning of the inner person with the great mysteries and secrets that are around us. It is the belief in the goodness of life and the possibility for each human person to contribute goodness to it. It is the belief in life as part of the eternal stream of time, that each of us came from somewhere and is destined to somewhere, that without such belief there could be no prayer, no meditation, no peace, and no happiness.[32]

Those words struck a deep core with me, representing a way to encapsulate a feeling, a sense of being in the world without any religious label. I believe what U Thant articulates is soul-knowing. In a strange and ethereal way, I could feel spirituality in the energy exchanges while embracing Muller's hands. It became conscious to me at that moment that I had experienced the same thing embracing Mario Montessori's hands and much earlier in my life, the hands of Ruth Gloria's Father Divine.

As I have said, throughout my childhood, adolescence, and early adult life, I felt like a I did not fit into the dominant paradigm. It was a very long journey to begin to understand that this fish needed to discover other waters. From my earliest memories there was a feeling of something not being right "out there." The *out there*, as I have come to know it, were the reactions of the dominant culture, including family, friends, and especially teachers. I was a sensitive child, and it was very difficult for me to fit into the mold our culture uses to shape the lives of young people.

Unfortunately, this kind of reality is often underneath the surface, encased by conditioning. We are all born as spiritual beings. For me that spiritual essence was slowly conditioned and encased by a culture of parents and relatives who were first generation children of Eastern European immigrants. How many times did I hear the adults in my life say, "Who the hell do you think you are?" The *me* of inner reflection, of why questions, of intense sensitivity to criticism and embarrassment, was not able to flower. At the same time, I was belligerent with authority at home and in school – standing up for right-action – which, in turn, resulted in more criticism and more embarrassment.

Perhaps my early soul's work was to experience sensitivity that would prepare me for my life's work. Perhaps that is why an angel in the form of Ruth Gloria befriended and watched over me during the extremely difficult pre-adolescent and adolescent years. And maybe living with an emotionally troubled sister – one who was never, as Fred Rogers would have it, "perfect just as she was" – gave me insight into caring for those who do not yet have their own voice.

In my late 20s things began to shift when my children entered Montessori school. I have to thank my first wife, Dolores, for insisting and then dragging me to parent meetings, which put me on the road to being aware of my own conditioning. Knowledge and understanding in and of itself was not enough to trump that conditioning. Earlier I told the story about my 4-year-old son being "too sensitive." The statement was not made in a tone that suggested approval. In fact, I was worried about his sensitivity. It is interesting that at that stage of my life, I had not yet reflected deeply about my own childhood and how sensitive I was to the world around me. Through the hearts of my children an inner transformation was changing my landscape and I begin making psychological and philosophical breakthroughs that led me from engineering to teaching. By my late 20s, illusions shattered, I began making conscious choices to expand that awareness and follow my heart.

———————◇———————

My friendships with three Montessorians – Mary Loew, David Trower, and Don Jenny – introduced me to a world of meaningful kinship. Our dialogue focused mainly on their Montessori experiences. From these interactions I gleaned that Montessori was not merely a method of education; it was a spiritual approach to life that had the potential to change the way human beings live – from self-centered and material values to altruism, peace, and collaboration.

The person guiding those early parent meetings was Mary Loew. I do not have immediate recall of the content of her comments; what I do know is that they must have resonated deeply because over the next 50 years I would establish a very close relationship with Mary, first as my mentor and later as peer and kindred spirit. In her role as Montessori teacher trainer she knew all the leaders of the movement, and it was her initiative that established my first contacts with the Montessori family. We were not only professional colleagues but also personal friends who explored life together. Mary definitely came into my river of influences at a critical junction in my journey as our personal and professional exploration flowed together from the mid-'70s through the late '80s. We remain close friends today.

Don enabled the fire to be lit in my heart when I uttered the words "Someday I might like to be a Montessori teacher," followed by an absolute soaring of awareness when Don's response was "Why not now?" In Joseph Campbell's "Hero's Journey," he identifies the initial phase of the journey as *separation*. Although I had been *separating* for five years this was the moment when I jumped off the edge, trusting that absolute good would manifest through the decision to become a Montessori teacher. In the map of my Great River, this is a time of sliding down the rapids.

Campbell names the second phase *initiation*. During the year of Montessori study at Bergamo, Italy, I was introduced to and immersed in a new paradigm, which has Cosmic Education as its cornerstone. My Great River meandered through new concepts and a new definition of self. I returned from Europe with a suitcase full of teaching and philosophy manuals – over 700 pages – as physical evidence. These notebooks were typed every day after the lectures and were accompanied by hand-drawn illustrations. More importantly, in my heart there was an inner knowing, a confirmation for my spiritual awareness of life.

Return is the third stage of Campbell's "Hero's Journey." During the *return*, the hero shares what he has learned. This is the Great River's entry into the ocean of life with the realization that the ocean has many ports of call, one of which may lead to another *separation*. The next "*separation*" came for me 15 years later when I left the organized Montessori community to eventually establish TIES and GATE. I have been engaging children and adults for nearly 50 years in iterations on the themes that I discovered at Bergamo.

In recent times I have been re-reading many of the books that Maria Montessori wrote while she was in India from 1939 to 1946. In the *Absorbent Mind* she says:

> Love is more than the electricity, which lightens our darkness, more than the etheric waves that transmit our voices across space, more than any of the energies that humanity has discovered and learned to use. Of all things, love is most potent.[33]

and

> One is tempted to say that the children are performing spiritual exercises, having found the path of self-perfecting and ascent to the inner heights of the soul. Their work, in its development, reminds one of the principles to be found in the Indian book of wisdom, the Bhagavad Gita.[34]

What did she find in the Gita? I think she was pointing to "Chapter 6 verse 5:

Lift up the self by the Self
And don't let it droop down,
For the Self is the self's only friend
And the self is the Self's only foe. "[35]

Still exploring what is underneath the underneath, Montessori's reference to the Gita brought me full circle to understanding her deep wisdom. In her earlier years she was so overwhelmed by her discoveries that she relied heavily on religious metaphors identifying the new children as Christlike. Her Indian experiences expanded and supported her understanding of what she had achieved.

Eknath Easwaren in *The Bhagavad Gita* explains:

The Rishis of ancient India analyzed their awareness of human experience to see if there was anything they found to be an absolute. Their findings can be summarized in three statements, which Aldous Huxley, following Leibnitz, has called the perennial philosophy because they appear in every age and every civilization: 1. There is an infinite, changeless reality beneath the world of change, 2. This same reality lies at the very core of every human personality, 3. The purpose of life is to discover this reality experientially: that is, to realize God while here on Earth.[36]

Aldous Huxley actually included two more: "That it is possible for human beings to love, know and to become actually identified with the Ground," as well as "That to achieve this unitive knowledge, to realize this supreme identity, is the final end and purpose of human existence."[37]

These words and ideas expressed by Huxley summarize so much about my own journey. Of course I did not have the vocabulary as a child, not even as a young adult, but I had the feelings that lay underneath… the search for oneness, for final cause, for Love. It did not come as a surprise to me that Maria Montessori would identify with the Gita. I already knew she had a spiritual, mystical understanding of cosmic consciousness. I could see that understanding, not only in her words from books and lectures but also in my own work with children and adults over the last 50 years. And I had the privilege of knowing many people who knew her, including her son, Mario, grandson Mario Jr., granddaughter, Renilde, Binda Goldsbrough, Maria Antonietta Paolini, Lena Wikramaratne, Abs Joosten, and Lakshmi Kripalani. Each had a deep reverence for Montessori whose presence was so charismatic. This reverence was also for an approach to education that might liberate teachers and learners so that they become catalysts for the *new human.*

———————◇———————

Walking amongst the trees this morning I caught a glimpse of how human life moves from feeling to seeing on the journey toward natural awareness.

Feeling is a sensory-emotional response to what-is. The Impressionist painters were responding to their environment in such a way, but it was so radical that they were hugely criticized (as "fish out of water") during the early years. As a young person I "felt" like that fish out of water; that is, I had this loosely assembled set of circumstances that made me feel that I did not belong in the movie I was in... and wondering why.

As I grew older and had some inspirational teachers, I would hear ideas and observe actions that touched me on an emotional level. It was the beginning of Seeing. Seeing is responding-noticing Truth and Right-Action. Seeing assuages doubt. As Seeing expands, it broadens personality, accepting "who I am" and noticing others "as they are." Clarity, as primordial awareness, is a first cousin to Seeing. Clarity-emptiness is the selfless state of pure and natural awareness.

Natural awareness is the presence of clarity-emptiness. It is not a point of arrival. Without a history of conditioning, young children experience this clarity-emptiness during the early years in Montessori environments. The prepared environment for children from birth to 6 years of age presents an opportunity for educating and discriminating all the senses in order to establish a concrete-tangible reality that enables the child to connect with the world as well as self in-the-world. It is a blossoming of awareness, which is a prerequisite for comprehending Ground later in life.

Natural awareness is noticing *what-is* without preconception, without separation of self and other. As early childhood moves on, it becomes the journey toward a state of extended connection to all that is, where contradiction becomes an opportunity to explore more deeply and where self, other, and life are a unity.

Loving awareness takes natural awareness to a cosmic level. It is the human quality that embraces the spark of creation in every form – the crystal bead that is and reflects *Isness* as Indra's net. I catch glimpses of this in the forest, at the beach, and in meditation, and every so often it emerges in dialogue. I have seen the latter in exchanges between students and faculty in our integrative learning coursework. The Montessori prepared environment for children from 6 to 12 is a time to sow the seeds for loving awareness through cosmic stories. Loving awareness can be intentional reflective moments whilst working with adolescents who are, in a manner of speaking, budding philosophers.

I take note that Montessori's work was influenced by the French philosopher Henri Bergson and the American philosopher William James. Aldous Huxley in his 1955 essay, "Who We Are" writes:

> Why is it that we think of ourselves as only this minute part of the totality far larger than we are – a totality, which according to many philosophers may actually be coextensive with the total activity of the universe? In the West you can go back as far as Leibniz with his conception that every monad was potentially omniscient. And in modern times you have the same conception in Bergson and in William James, both of whom were of the opinion that the consciousness that we have is simply a kind of filtering down of some form of universal cosmic consciousness, narrowed down for the purpose of helping us survive biologically on the surface of this particular planet.[38]

In this chapter I explored The Great River as a metaphor for observing inner and outer movements on one's life journey. My own river of awareness has interconnected with so many significant people who have helped me view underneath the underneath. Looking back, Ruth Gloria, Marsha Morgan, and Maria Montessori have been the most significant influences in the river of my life.

———◇———

Part I has been an exploration of the experiences and events in my life that gave rise to the formation of the driving question articulated throughout Chapters One through Six. Written over the last eight years, Part II is an expression and response to that question, when creativity has been flowing freely in my river. This period of time has helped me begin to understand all that Marsha and I created over our 25 years of love and partnership. What I know for certain is that my peach tree has borne fruit. I invite you now to turn the page and sample what hangs from the tree.

PART TWO:
VISION

CHAPTER SEVEN:
NATURAL MAPPING

Living in a new way involves creating a worldview that sees humanity as a participant in the natural cycles of the Earth and subject to the laws of the Cosmos. This worldview implies deep regard for all of creation.[39] Marsha Morgan

I spend a substantial amount of time walking, meditating, and writing during my three weekly tramps through a four kilometer stretch of the Pacific Northwest forest. It is restorative as well as inspirational. I feel that spirit has drawn me to the trees throughout my life in order to reconnect to my soul's essence, providing me with a direct experience in the nature of life and the natural cycles that bring forth Earth's bounty, sustenance, and equilibrium.

I have always loved being amongst trees. Between 1998 and 2011 Marsha and I took several trips 400 km south from Christchurch, New Zealand to an area known as "The Catlins." The lushness of the greenery and dampness of the air was so pervasive that I could feel it inside of my body as we tramped through muddy trails, over small bridges, and across streams, stepping from stone to stone on our way to numerous waterfalls. On the Catlin east coast we observed penguin colonies and on the south coast we saw small icebergs that had broken free from Antarctica. We walked along the shallows where the Tasman Sea and South Pacific Ocean flow into each other. Submerged, 10 cm under the sea's edge, were the petrified remains of 250 million years ago (mya) Permian forests that joined with New Zealand when it separated from Gondwana 80 mya.

From a Western perspective, the field of ecology was born some 2400 years ago when Aristotle or his student, Theophrastus, described their observation of interrelationships between animals and their environments. Throughout the 20th century, scientific discoveries revealed the facts behind the inextricable web of interconnections found on Earth. Most notable was the work of Vladimir Vernadsky, who in the 1920s developed the concept of biosphere as a "life sphere" or global ecological system of systems where life resides. The term had formally been coined in 1875 by Eduard Suess: the place on Earth's surface where life dwells.

Looking at ecology from an Eastern perspective, 4000 years ago the Vedic seers had a sense of deep gratitude for Mother Earth. The Vedic hymns[40] are filled with many simple but universal messages, such as:

- Plants are mothers and Goddesses. (Rig Veda Samhita x-97-4)
- Sacred grass has to be protected from man's exploitation. (Rig Veda Samhita vii-75-8)
- Plants and waters are treasures for generations. (Rig Veda Samhita vii-70-4)
- We invoke all supporting Earth on which trees, lords of forests, stand ever firm. (Atharva Veda 12:1:27)
- Do not cut trees because they remove pollution. (Rig Veda 6:48:17)

And in the *Bhagavad Gita* (400 BCE), "Krishna compares the world to a single banyan tree with unlimited branches, where all species of animals, humans and demigods wander."[41] The context for this insight in the Gita may have arisen from the epic poem Indra's Net, written 1000 years earlier and referred to in the Hindu *Atharva Veda*.

It was not until the latter part of the 20th century that the ecological or environmental movement evolved, advocating a sustainable approach to living within the resource limits of our planet. No one did more to shift the world stage than scientist Rachel Carson, whose 1962 book, *Silent Spring,* sounded the first major alarm that human activity was having a destabilizing effect on the sustainable nature of life on Earth. Ten years later, influenced by Carson's writing, Norwegian philosopher Arne Ness coined the words *deep ecology,* launching a global environmental movement.

A few years later microbiologist Lynn Margulis and chemist, James Lovelock, authored the Gaia hypothesis, which postulates that all organisms within the Earth systems are integrated to form one self-regulating complex. In the early days it was known as "the Earth is alive" or Gaia Hypothesis. With more and more scientific proof, this hypothesis was elevated to the status of theory during the 1990s.

My own connection to ecology began in the garden. With Ruth Gloria as my guide, between the ages of 10 and 16 I planted vegetable gardens and learned to talk with the plants as I had seen Ruth do so often. During these years of growing up I lived in Forest Hills, New York, amongst the pin oaks, maples, and ginkgo trees. Our home was adjacent to Forest Hills Gardens, an area of deep wooded lots surrounding beautiful houses. Indeed I grew up inside a forest within the perimeter of New York City.

The Montessori journey deeply connects children to Earth and sustainable principles through Cosmic Education, which has as its keynote the reality that everything in the cosmos is interconnected through a synergistic web of existence. During the late '60s and early '70s Maria Montessori's son, Mario, lectured at Bergamo, Italy on the concept of Ecology. In 1971, nine years after Rachel Carson's seminal book, Mario Montessori, Sr. explained:

> In the Biosphere there is no isolation. All things, which form the environment, are connected. After all studies are done it can be affirmed that all the Earth and Cosmos from the micro to the macro-organism are completely joined and bound. In order to understand ecology, we must see the environment as a main factor in the development and formation of life. Neither plant nor animal can be independent of its environment. The word

ecology comes from "aikor" which means dwelling place and "logos" means idea. Ecology can be studied anywhere from the Polar Regions to the tropics, from the depths of the oceans to the top of the mountains. It may be studied in every forest, plain, lake, sea or pond. These things have their own ecosystem. The entire biosphere is an ecosystem and then this is divided into smaller and smaller ecosystems.[42]

When Marsha and I joined personal and professional lives in the early '90s, we came together holding Gaia and Cosmos. It was a natural evolution to our eco-cosmological approach to education and life.

—————◇—————

Please join with me as I walk through the forest...

I stand in a small opening with sunlight trickling through the branches. Tryon Creek flows nearby and I can hear the water thrashing its way around the rocks. The sounds of crow and raven, hawk and woodpecker, and other songbirds are often present. The forest floor is teeming with life as I observe slugs, beetles, worms, squirrels and, every once in a while, I see deer or fox and hear coyote howl. The entire forest is saturated with living beings that depend on each other for survival. This is the nature of an ecosystem. The primary condition for this ecosystem to survive is the health of its soil. A nourishing soil celebrates life; an undernourished one diminishes life. In a natural system the soil may be identified as the stability or maintenance function.

Tryon Creek Forest is a region within the Tryon Creek watershed in Southwest Portland, Oregon, which lies in the geographical region known the Pacific Northwest. As we increase the magnitude of our perspective, people begin to view the Earth as a whole – the geosphere upon which we live, the matrix function that embodies form and relationship.

Back in the Tryon Creek Forest I am immediately aware of the fresh sweet pungent stream of air. I thank the living-breathing trees for taking carbon dioxide from the atmosphere and giving back oxygen. I remember studying photosynthesis in high school and reading textbooks with mechanical illustrations. There is no comparison to sitting in the forest and taking deep breaths to clear mind and heart. My dearest friends, Oak and Cedar, absorb the moisture from the soil, water from the creek and a deluge of rain from October through April. This area of the United States is a designated rainforest. The interplay of water and air, hydrosphere and atmosphere, is the basis for the "partnership function" in a natural system.

The science of the 20th century revealed the very nature of how elements cycle through life in communities of oxygen, carbon, nitrogen, phosphorous, and sulfur, as well as the mega water and rock cycles. Earth systems science tells the story of all the bio-geological cycles that penetrate our living planet. These cycles as a whole are known as the unity function in a natural system as their activity enables the component functions to work together synchronously.

Flowing through all the niches of Tryon Creek Forest is a network of producers, consumers – predator and prey relationships – that enable the forest to sustain itself. This is the food web in our natural system and is sometimes called the feedback function.

Springtime, when the trillium begins to shoot and flower, the emergence of new life conjures images of a ballet in slow motion. The Earth's biosphere encompasses the evolution of life and represents the growth function in natural systems.

Thus far I have identified

…the soil as the stability-maintenance function

…the geosphere as the matrix function

…the atmosphere and hydrosphere as the partnership function

…the bio-geological cycles as the unity function

…the food webs as the feedback function

…and the biosphere as the growth function.

The light and heat that emanate from our sun (Heliosphere) provides Earth-Gaia with energy that is the stimulant for all of the other functions.

Using the *Our Planet, Our Home*[43] illustrations, the following image, shown in Figure 1, depicts the above relationships.

Figure 1. Gaian System Relationships

Marsha, a gardener and permaculturist by nature, was drawn to explore these relationships in profound ways, developing a process she named *natural mapping*. Natural maps help one see how ecological systems are interdependent. Figure 2 shows the map she developed which shows the functions mentioned above.

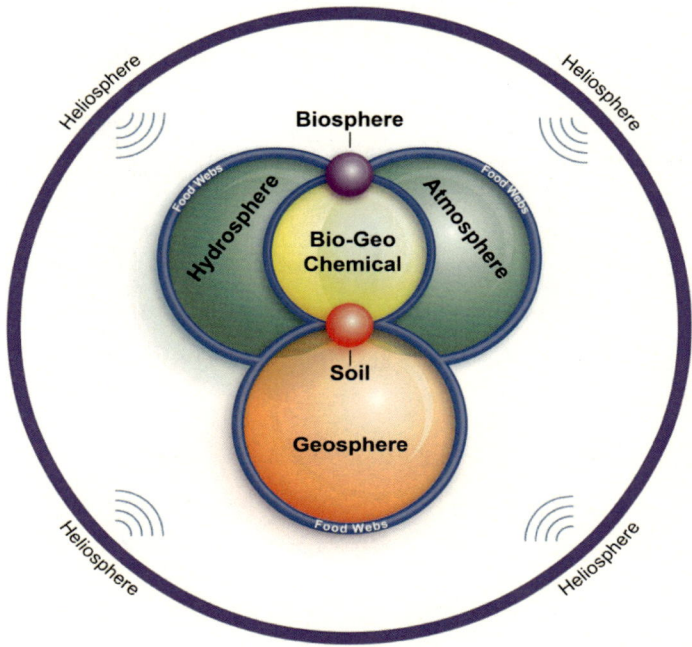

Figure 2. Natural Map of Gaian System Relationships

To lessen resistance to the science of natural mapping, I invite people to *grok* these concepts. Grok is a word, coined by Robert Heinlein in his 1961 science fiction novel *Stranger in a Strange Land*. To grok means to understand intuitively without analysis.

———————◇———————

In the early 1990s, physicist and systems scientist, Fritjof Capra, established The Elmwood Institute to explore an ecological framework that might lead to a new approach to teaching ecology in schools. Elmwood identified eight components to the systemic view of ecological relationships:

   1. The unity function: *What integrates the whole?* For the Earth, these are the bio-geochemical cycles.

2 and 3. The partnership functions: *What two systems work together as a duality expressing unity?* The atmosphere and the hydrosphere engage in an exchange of competition and cooperation.

4. The matrix function: *What medium or structure is needed for Earth systems' survival?* The lithosphere (or geosphere) is the resource base defining the carrying capacity for all of Earth's systems.

5. The stability-maintenance function: *What ensures the continuity of the system?* All living systems must maintain themselves to ensure the system's stability and continuity. For the Earth, this is the soil.

6. The feedback function: *What function flows through all the others to balance stability and growth?* All living systems contain complex feedback patterns. For the Earth, this is represented by food webs.

7. The growth function: *What processes provide change, creativity, and direction for the system?* For the Earth, life itself — as it catalyzes dynamic change in every part of the system.

8. The energy function: *What is the external source of energy?* All living systems are powered by an external source of energy. For Gaia, it is the sun.

As will be shared in Chapter Ten, the above Natural Map representation of Gaian Community depicts, in the absence of hierarchy, the integrated dynamics of holarchical systems within holarchical systems. The map that follows (see Figure 3) names the eight functions. I will use this natural mapping approach in subsequent sections of this book.

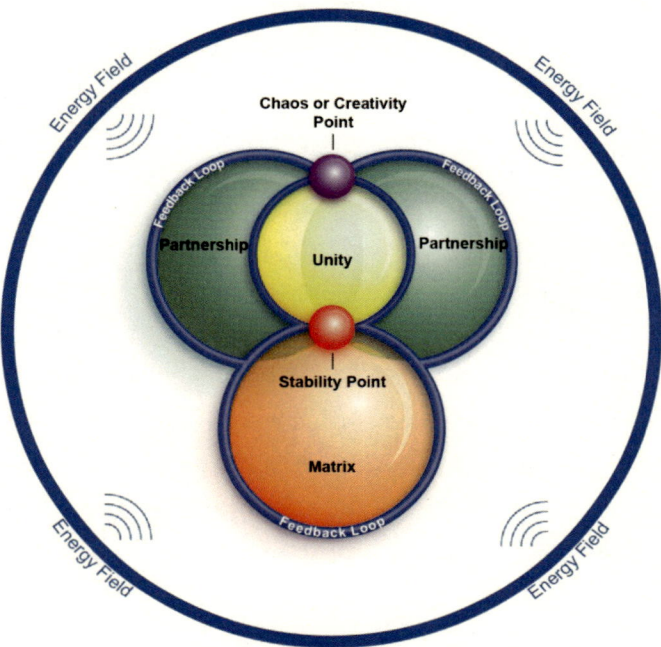

Figure 3. Natural Map of Gaian Community Functions

Marsha did not stop here. She expanded on the ecosystem perspective by applying the same ideas to the nature of human systems in order to discover how organizations, governments, social structures or even personal relationships might be explored to understand their potential for sustainability. This extends the ideas of Capra and Luisi:

> The key to an operational definition of ecological sustainability is the realization that we do not need to invent sustainable human communities from scratch but can model them after nature's ecosystems, which *are* sustainable communities of plants, animals, and microorganisms.[44]

In thinking deeply about this approach, I have realized that as natural systems-relationships occur here on Earth they are also present within a larger context. The Earth is a derivative of all that evolution has provided. So it is that the Universe is organized in such a way that our galaxy is a network of interdependent systems, and similarly so for clusters of galaxies and for the cosmos as a whole.

In Chapter Nine, *"To Educate Eco-Sapiens,"* I name and explain this holonic view of organization.

Marsha and I used a systemic, natural mapping technique to explore issues like the structure of a school or organization of an academic inquiry. We even used it to explore personal relationship questions. For us it provided a way of applying ecological-sustainable vision principles to the organization of any set of contexts. I have been playing with how I might use the natural mapping process to identify the core contexts and processes explored in this book. These are always a work in process. For today, a quintessential spring afternoon in a Northwest rainforest, these are my thoughts.

The unity function – the Indra's Net of this book – is integrative learning as well as the Montessori vision. These core contexts contain the thought processes and experiences that become the threads, which weave all the elements together.

Cosmos and Gaia are the partnership function circles. The cosmic perspective and integral relationships with Gaia are primary and coupled in this exploration.

The matrix or resource base in this natural map is a spiritual approach to life, one that embraces an exploration of the ground, transcendent, and the imminent.

Right-action and love hold the position of the stability point. It is the paramount focus of my driving question.

I placed dialogue and questioning in the interconnected circles that form the feedback function. The art of identifying core questions and using dialogue to explore them with others in the learning community is an essential key to educating for right-action and love.

The growth function represents change and creativity. For this book, and its emphasis on the evolution of the new human being, I name it the future of humanity.

Universal love is the cosmic energy that drives this inquiry.

Figure 4 shows the natural map of *Educating for Right-Action and Love: Extending and Expanding the Montessori Vision:*

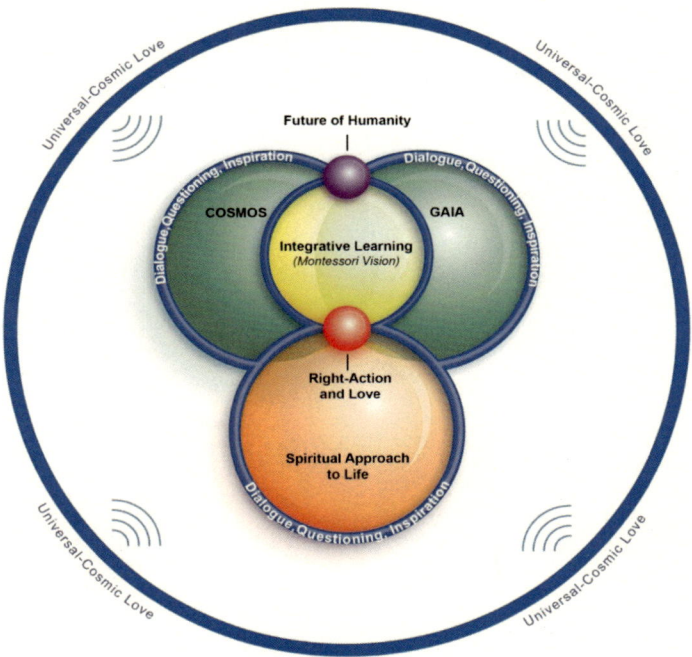

Figure 4. Natural Map of Educating for Right-Action and Love

This natural map is a contextual perception of how I envision the interrelationships emerge in educating for right-action and love. It is dynamic, rather than static, with each aspect noting a journey, rather than a point of arrival. Marsha developed this process, which she referred to in her thesis:

> The process of using dynamical systems to model human process traces a long history from the time of Newton and his calculus.

One of its names is Erodynamics [In the field of mathematics and chaos theory]. It is used to create human social and cultural forms reflectively and consciously. The dynamical systems view that I employ is an adaptation and is no longer a strictly mathematical model. It is a model that jogs our thinking and creates a vocabulary to reflect upon the arrangements that we make with one another. It is a symbol, a tool. We are asked to Grok the model rather than analyze it.[45]

Inherent in its way of constructing meaning, natural mapping embodies motion, movement; it is verb-like. Grokked as a whole, one of the keynotes of right-action and love is peace through education.

CHAPTER EIGHT:
PEACE THROUGH EDUCATION[46]

> *By taking good care of the present moment,*
> *we take good care of the future.*
> *Working for peace in the future is to*
> *work for peace in the present moment.*
> Thich Nhat Hanh[47]

The overarching question that gave energy to the creation of this book is:

> *What contexts and processes in education might liberate teachers and*
> *learners so that they become catalysts for a "new human" — one whose*
> *integral relationship with Gaia is bound by right-action and love?*

Peace through education responds to that question.

During the rocky 1960s while working for the largest military contractor in the United States and when civil rights and anti-war demonstrations were at their peak, I had the insight that education was the only way to lessen these crises. Educating would need a totally new form in order to give rise to a totally new humanity, one capable of creating a more just and peaceful civilization. Soon after that recognition, I left engineering to become a teacher.

Today my driving questions for peace through education are: *What is the influence of dialogue on the process of peace? What is the relationship between inner and outer peace? In what ways might the former be a prerequisite for the latter? How can teacher-learners and learner-teachers create an atmosphere of peacing? What are the spiritual qualities that embrace peace as an ongoing soul experience?*

Recently I have been exploring the idea of changing some of my favorite nouns into verbs. Nouns freeze time whereas verbs are in-process. There is no verb "to peace," so peace has a quality of thingness; it can be objectified. It is a state at rest – an historical point, a present experience, or a future target. What if peace were a verb? A person might experience peacing as a continuous journey bringing awareness to his or her inner world while peacing with others.

What does it mean "to peace"? Is peace of mind simply the absence of conflict? As a thinker with a philosophical bent, I find the concept of peace of mind to be alluring. In fact, at times in my life, I have experienced what I consider peace of mind. Yet those moments slip quickly into the past when thoughts, particularly binding, non-progressive thoughts arise, reminding me of that which is "not yet" at peace. My worry list intercedes, and I can lose my stability.

Binding and non-progressive thoughts are ones that create emotional storms. They are based on conditioned responses and can take me into tunnels of doubt-fear. Even if I mitigate the prominent worry, it may soon be replaced by another, as mind-thought is encased in its own conditioning.

What if you could immediately recognize a binding thought and the resistance it creates *before* doubt or fear arise? In feeling the emotion attached to that thought, you might say, "That is interesting," without having to find a remedy, only *observing* in order to *see*. By becoming consciously aware of my in and out breath, I have discovered that the practice of mindfulness provides a buffer to binding thoughts, sometimes transforming them for increased awareness. It does not always work. Short circuits occur when stress brings me back to highly tense moments, like living though 25 earthquakes greater than 5.0 within 24 months or the residual stress from caretaking for my wife during a very unstable period of her Alzheimer's progression. At moments that trigger stress, sometimes binding, emotional memory overcomes practice.

I see peacing as an inner process where one experiences fluidity around the unanticipated adventures of life. Buddhists would call this "unchanging wakefulness."

> *Respond to the What-Is*
> *by seeing, pausing*
> *and seeing again;*
> *pausing*
> *and seeing again.*

Peacing through education calls out to teacher-educators to be in relationship with their own inner peace dialogue. By necessity, then, the process of teacher preparation has to be congruent with the desired outcomes. We have to live the practice that we advocate in the teaching-learning process. Peace is *not* the objective; it is not an end in itself. Peace is a process of fulfilling the divine consciousness that each human receives. Peace is driven by right-action and its qualities include gratitude, compassion-empathy, humility, patience, and love.

As an engineer, I saw myself as a liberal in a sea of conservatives. During a workplace meeting, I remember listening closely to the communication exchanges and that old childhood feeling of being a fish that could not swim in that water came welling up inside. I distinctly remember thinking, "*There is something wrong here. I do not belong.*" Around me I felt an atmosphere of mistrust, competition, and fear. I wondered where these attitudes originated and how that could shift. Might education be the source of this sort of conditioning?

As explained earlier, protesters against the Vietnam War and for Civil Rights enveloped me. I didn't march, but I was with them heart and soul. Dissonance between who I understood myself to be and my engineering career increased. I reached the conclusion that there was no way forward for humanity unless the nature of teaching and learning was transformed. This thought stayed with me as I became more active as a parent at my children's Montessori school.

Something felt absolutely "right" about that experience. I became friends with the teachers who spoke a language that captured my ideological heart.

In my youth I knew about peace as the absence of war. I had no concept that peace might be an inner process. That came much later when, in my late twenties, Spirit introduced me to philosophy and states of consciousness. I have been dancing with the idea of peace as a way of life – an inner journey – for more than 50 years. Life experiences, especially in relationships and through teaching and learning with both children and adults, have shown me that peace is multifaceted and challenging to maintain.

Awareness of my inner processes amplified and was forever internalized as I tended to Marsha during her cognitive decline. The four years before she went into full-time care were filled with loss and protection. Those experiences enabled me to be acutely aware of observing and noticing "that which is important." It also left me with an understanding of the deep beauty we shared – teaching me about love and peace in the most profound way.

I have also been influenced by the teachings of Jiddu Krishnamurti whose insight into personal transformation comes through an understanding that "truth is a pathless land,"[48] and that each person has to observe his or her own conditioning in order to *see*.

Another influence was U.N. Assistant Secretary-General Robert Muller, whom I met in New York in 1984. During our dialogue, he introduced me to the work of Thomas Berry and Brian Swimme. I first met Berry at the *Seeking the True Meaning of Peace* conference in Costa Rica and later visited him at his home in New York. Swimme and I have had ongoing contact for nearly 20 years.

Having survived two world wars, Muller wrote the book *Most of All They Taught Me Happiness*. I invited Muller to be one of the keynote presenters at a Montessori 1985 AMI international study conference that I co-organized. The conference was titled *Education and Peace*. His lecture was titled *Peace, Spirituality and Global Education*. When he became Chancellor for the U.N. University for Peace, he invited me for dialogues at the university's home in Costa Rica. Muller says that, "It is our paramount duty to educate children in the art of living and happiness, in believing in humanity's success and the establishment of a peaceful, just, brotherly and happy world."[49]

Naturally, the work of Maria Montessori was a very strong influence. In 1917, after visiting World War I refugee camps in France and Italy, Montessori was alarmed by the suffering of children, not just from physical injury, but also and more so from psychic injury. In her peace lectures, she called for the creation of a White Cross that would assuage "a special form of mental disturbance, which constitutes a real mental wound – a lesion that is as serious, if not more serious than wounds of the physical body."[50] The White Cross would work alongside the Red Cross and be staffed by teachers that were trained in her methods in order to create environments that would lead to normalization. The *Washington Post* published an article on March 8, 2018 titled "How to Help Syria's Refugee Children." The author, Erica Moretti, reminds readers that there may be a helpful solution for the refugee children. She says, "More than a century ago, the Italian educator Maria Montessori argued for confronting the psychological devastation of children of war with a robust education program. She conceived of the idea of an entire organization to provide such a service: The White Cross."[51]

Montessori travelled throughout Europe during the 1930s lecturing at international conferences addressing her observations that only through a new education could a new human arise to create a peaceful and just society. She came to that realization after 25 years of observing the personality changes in children who attended her schools. Montessori was not an advocate for teaching peace per se, but more so for creating peaceful learning environments, infused with ethical and moral contexts. She continued her focus on peace whilst lecturing in India during the 1940s. In 1949, 1950, and 1951 Montessori was nominated for the Nobel Peace Prize.

In my work with children and adults, I experience teaching as a facilitation process that is imbued with unconditioning. "Peace" is something that permeates the environment. It is the way we interact with learners, the way we help them explore differences. This approach will result in a more peaceful civilization, not because peace was taught, but because peacing was lived through dialogue.

Speaking at the Montessori Training College in 1931, Mahatma Gandhi recognized Maria Montessori's understanding about peace through education:

> You have very truly remarked that "if we are to reach real peace in this world and if we are to carry on a real war against war, we shall have to begin with children." If they grow up in their natural innocence, we won't have the struggle, we won't have to pass fruitless idle resolutions, but we shall go from love to love and peace to peace, until at last all the corners of the world are covered with that peace and love for which, consciously or unconsciously, the whole world is hungering.[52]

Montessori's ideas for peaceful social change were not limited to education. During the 1930s she called for the Social Party of the Child, to give children a voice and representation in all the parliaments of the world.

During our more than twenty years as partners in love and work, Marsha taught me much about peacemaking. Observing her with both children and adults was a window and a mirror into a new way of being. I smile now as I recall the day I was rather stern with some reticent 10-year-olds who were not doing what they were "supposed" to be doing. Marsha whispered in my ear, "You know, they're just children." A rush of letting go tethered through my body.

In the last chapter I explored the Natural Mapping process. I have applied those concepts to integrating my thoughts on peace through education and eight aspects emerge that may foster the development of both inner and outer peace in an educational setting:

Unconditioning

Normalizing

Prepared Environment, Integrative Learning, and Systems Thinking

Right-Action and Love

Attention, Noticing, Observation, Reflection, Meditation,

and Contemplation

Dialogue

Peace as a Verb

Spiritual Awareness and Cosmic Worldview

This Natural Map of Peace through Education (Figure 5) demonstrates that all eight aspects are contextual — derived from weaving parts into a whole.

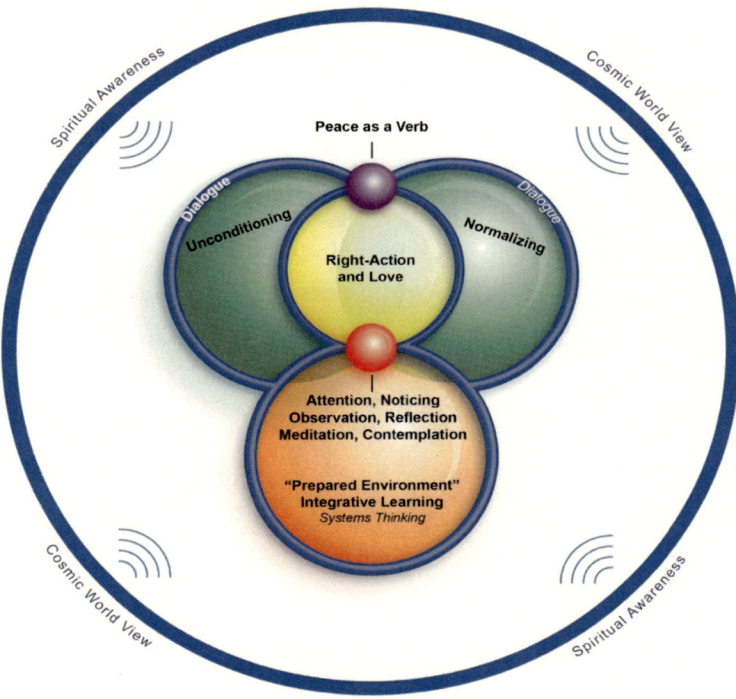

Figure 5. Natural Map of Peace through Education

The place to begin the exploration is with ***unconditioning***. Together with ***normalizing*** they form the *partnership function.*

Krishnamurti spent his life exploring the domain of psychological freedom. There is an ancestral and cultural imprint that prejudices, or conditions the mind, resulting in unexamined assumptions about life. He asserts that to rid oneself of these assumptions is freedom's gateway and the essential task of education. He names the process *unconditioning*. Krishnamurti explains:

> The question is whether (the teacher) and the student in their relationship in a school can uncondition themselves?
>
> [Is it] possible to educate human beings, from childhood and beyond, to cultivate, to nurture the whole outward and inward totality of [each person]. That is, for me, right-education. Is it possible in our life to educate ourselves completely, totally, inwardly as well as outwardly?[53]

Unconditioning begins when we pay attention to our thinking patterns in order to *observe* coherence with right-love and right-action. These patterns of thought have psychological, cultural, or philosophical roots. Exploratory questioning is an inner and outer dialogue that may transform conditioning. These are questions "worth thinking about" and take a different direction based on the developmental stage of the learner. Endicott College-TIES M.Ed. graduate, Aarthi Nandakumar explains, "The ideologies and philosophies discussed as a part of this program led me to question a lot of my previously held assumptions and look at things from a fresh perspective."[54]

Stories are an essential container in the unconditioning process. They provide a sense of wonder and appreciation for the significance of life. They offer questions and metaphors to comprehend mystery, and they identify the overarching contexts that shape who we are.

Normalizing is the process of restoring the circumstances prior to conditioning that compromise the psyche. It is a term used in psychotherapy and bodywork. Maria Montessori employed it to address the qualities she observed in children attending her schools. It is inner development characterized by the emergent traits of deep concentration; collaboration; biophilia; love of work; love of repetition; empathy; humility; compassion; independence; cooperation; and love of silence.

These traits reveal themselves in a "prepared" learning environment that supports freedom of choice in an atmosphere where learners and educators mutually embrace right-action and love. I observed these traits throughout my years of working with children. However, I did not realize that adults could also be in a normalizing process. At the end of her graduate journey in our master's program, Alison Jones says: "*I have discovered that my personal beliefs and professional beliefs are aligned and this gives me great peace. I have discovered that my role as an educator is to observe the needs of my students and respond appropriately.*"[55]

The *resource base* or *matrix* for Peace through Education is a prepared learning environment imbued by integrative learning and systems thinking.

A ***prepared environment*** is a setting that maximizes the growth of independence, as participants have freedom to explore activities for inner and outer development. It not only emphasizes the physical setting and mental acquisition of knowledge, but it is also imbued with the qualities of love and reflective awareness. For these qualities to evolve, educator-teachers have a compelling need to engage their own inner peace dialogue.

Integrative learning and systems thinking are reciprocal processes. In Fritjof Capra's *Web of Life* he explains:

> By the 1930s most of the key criteria of systems thinking had been formulated by biologists, psychologists, and ecologists. In all these fields the exploration of living systems – organisms, parts of organisms, and communities of organisms – has led scientists to the same new way of thinking in terms of connectedness, relationships, and context.[56]

From a scientific view, integrative learning is a derivative of systems thinking. However, integrative learning is much more; it is a context for the integration of heart, body, mind, and soul. In that way it is a spiritual practice. It is also a container for normalizing and unconditioning. It recognizes strategies and approaches, such as: creative expression, non-adversarial relationships, acknowledging intuitionheart wisdom, and the formation of dynamic learning communities, as well as exploration based on personal interest. TIES graduate, Hiba Hijazi explains:

> Systems thinking helped me in my work and in my daily life. In spite of being discouraged sometimes when I find my ideas differing greatly from those who are around in my community, I now feel excited to observe the outcomes of this new emerging mode of thinking.[57]

The journey of inner knowing embraces the deep over-arching context that *all is one*: one Universe – one cosmos – one Earth community. To perpetuate that oneness, humans need to live within the ecological carrying capacity of the Earth. The *unity function* in this Peace through Education Natural Map is held by Right-Action and Love.

Right-action is our ethical contract with life. When we act "rightly," we act without selfish attachment. We act mindfully. Our "right" actions spring from love, compassion, and understanding.

Love is *a priori* for peace because it is a container for unconditional acceptance, as well as a continuum of respect and reverence for life and the unfolding potential of humanity. Without love, learning is reduced to a method or a subject, and the field of experience is limited. Universal love parallels universal responsibility. It emanates from a core understanding and visceral experience of evolution, as well as humanity's place in the natural order. Embedded in love is the quality of gratitude. Indian spiritual teacher Sri Chinmoy writes: "Peace is the beginning of love. / Peace is the completion of truth. / Peace is the return to the source."[58]

The *focal or stability point* in this natural map of peace through education recognizes that a person needs space and quiet time for *Attention, Noticing, Observation, Reflection, Meditation, and Contemplation*. All these attributes might be replaced with one word, *mindfulness*, as they represent the "pause" that can erase conditioned responses and allow love and right-action to emerge. They set the context for living a life that seeks truth and practices compassion.

Dialogue holds the *feedback space* for integrating flow. It is a method of exchange within a learning community that carries active intention. Dialogue is a process that begins with a willingness to be tentative about what you know, and its focus is on what-is rather than on ideas and opinions. It allows communication to unfold with affection and mutual support as well as respect. Therefore, dialogue is the process of communication in a non-adversarial learning environment. Its purpose is to pursue shared meaning.

Aarthi Nandakumar's reflections also include the following thoughts:

The evidence that dialogue is a beautiful way to communicate comes from how I feel about the space of communication. It touched my soul because in a dialogue, people are non-judgmental, open and receptive to feedback, and hence I had no fear to express my thoughts and emotions. This was in contrast to the previous education experiences. And that's why I always mention that this M.Ed. has been the true education of my life![59]

Peace as a verb is an unfolding process. It is not a static state or condition and holds the position of *change and growth* in this Natural Map. As mentioned earlier, peace is an inner process where one experiences fluidity around the vicissitudes of life. Participating in a learning community reflects the aspects of education that are addressed in this Natural Map of Peace through Education. TIES graduate, Molly Smith, explains:

This program creates a learning environment that takes the community's reflections on content, helping the individual to find deeper understanding. It is not set up to change an individual's mind, yet it is designed to encourage a thoughtful and tolerant environment. The program also helps TIES students understand the implications that this type of learning can and will have on future generations. It has created an awareness that has allowed me to become a stronger teacher to young children as well a competent earth community member. [60]

The sources of influence, the *energy function* in this natural map are ***spiritual awareness and a cosmic worldview***. In a 1939 letter from Maria Montessori to Mahatma Gandhi, Montessori says, "Spiritual attraction is the force that can save humanity. The art of spiritually approaching the child is a secret that can establish human brotherhood; it is a divine heart that will lead to the peace of humankind."[61]

The ***cosmic worldview*** acknowledges the ongoing journey of the Universe and the contextual relationships that are a derivative of that journey. In Cosmic Education learners may fall into bliss with existence. They are...

...in awe of creative emergence,

...notice natural and systemic relationships,

...and are aware of being aware.

And they are invited to discover their Cosmic Task or Great Work to honor their human responsibility.

Decades ago, I realized that the immense problems facing humanity could only be remedied through a new form of education – one that provided overarching contexts so that learners would come to know that everything is interconnected in a meticulous web of relationships. I believed that this knowledge would change the way we behave toward each other and toward the Earth. I was only partially right. *Knowledge itself is not enough.* There needs to be congruent, seamless processes that allow learners to live in those contexts and develop right-action. Those seamless processes are revealed in the Natural Map of Peace through Education. And Peace through Education responds to the driving question that put this book in your hands.

CHAPTER NINE:
GIVING BACK MONTESSORI
TO MONTESSORI

The children, with their simplicity of action,
work in harmony with the cosmos.
We [adults] must enter into harmony
and take up our own Cosmic Task.[62]
The revolutionary movements of our days
are a sign of the great crisis from which
"the universal consciousness"
of humanity is about to be born.[63]
Maria Montessori

In 1982, several months after Mario Montessori, Sr. passed away, his widow, Ada, sent a letter thanking me for organizing his last visit to the United States the year before. In an excerpt she writes, "I only feel that Mario had the real gift for pointing out the essence, and I am afraid people may lose themselves in the details." Nearly 40 years later I would have to concur with this foretelling. Although the movement has expanded, the roots are being lost to outcome-based learning. This chapter explores and nourishes those roots as it reveals Montessori's overarching vision for humanity.

As you have seen, my life's journey shaped and drew me into Montessori and then Montessori shaped my life. It has been a cosmic relationship of reciprocity and integration. In this chapter we explore the essence Ada Montessori referred to, which shines a light on Montessori's universal insights that apply in any educational setting.

After more than 50 years, I now have an expanded understanding of Maria Montessori's contributions for the well-being of humanity. Passing on her legacy is immensely critical for the harmonious development of civilization. Her life's focus was on a universal transformation that would be the result of educating for the rise of a *new human*. As we shall see, this vision became clearer during the 1930s and 1940s.

Maria Montessori's most significant attribute was her ability to observe *without prejudice* – without judgments or assumptions – free from conditioning. This was competence that she possessed right from the beginning. She challenged the old paradigm that relegated children to the "not yet." She had the capacity for the kind of instant *seeing* that Krishnamurti talks about. This kind of seeing does not require time; it is an immediate knowing of *what-is* from which right-action takes place.

What did she see? She saw that children need activity/work in order to develop their personality… and that this activity would help them absorb the culture by participating in it. (Although Montessori refers only to children, my experience is that all humans, regardless of age, need activity/work to develop their psychological well-being.) The emerging personality characteristics took her totally by surprise. She called it normalization and it spontaneously came to light when she applied her principles whilst working with ordinary children in the first Children's House (1907)[64]. The qualities of the normalizing process become the ground floor for the development of the abstract mind after 6 years of age. As I explain later in this chapter, after six years children can gain the abstract capacity for *seeing* that all life on Earth works to fulfill its needs and, in so doing, unconsciously gives back to the whole. For Montessori this began in the gardens and forests surrounding her accommodations in India and was followed by scientific contextual stories that strike the imagination of the child. Questions that trigger deep reflection like, "*What do you give back?*" can be placed on the table. And their minds can make the connection to Cosmic Task and Great Work. It was Montessori's intention that all the stories given to 6- to 12-year-old children would include this theme of cosmic generosity or giving back – even metaphorically. Geography, History, Biology, Zoology are not taught; they are experienced as interconnected aspects of the Cosmic Web.

What else did she see? Montessori saw immediately that children are *tomorrow in present time.* How they grow and learn will profoundly affect the future of humanity. This insight is critical. The formation of the adult begins at birth and that formation is dependent upon the kind of education engaged.

How did she translate this into action? She provided activities and exercises that would heighten the children's potential to satisfy their *needs* – physical, intellectual, social, emotional, and spiritual. One of Montessori's core observations was that "The mind is formed by abstractions that it has drawn from material things. Our material presents the abstractions in a materialized form."[65] The mind is also formed by activities that draw children into relationship with nature as well as each other. Contemplating flowers, trees, gardening, caring for animals, and observing beauty inspires awe and wonder while fostering gratitude and appreciation.

Lo and behold, in satisfying these needs, the children were set on a profound learning journey that included orientation toward self, other, and all life. The response to these experiences was not only inner joy but also a transformation of the personality – with emergent normalization traits such as deep concentration, collaboration, biophilia, love of work, love of repetition, empathy, humility, compassion, independence, cooperation, and love of silence. Montessori recalls the beginnings of her work, "We saw that natural relations with the environment were produced within the child and then superior moral qualities came to the surface, such as discipline, order in actions as well as order in feelings, including love.[66]

She believed this preparation during childhood would form the basis of a new social – and even universal – awareness that would set the course of humanity to align with our cosmic potential.

Just as I explored the roots of my own life to expose the origin of my driving question, I have wondered too about the catalysts in Montessori's life that set her on a lifetime of exploration to educate the human potential. What seeds were planted that gave birth to her intuitive wisdom? Did her parents have a determining influence? As a child we know she was quite sensitive to the needs of others – especially those less fortunate. Young Maria's attitude of "care and respect for others came from her mother Renilde."[67] Her father, Alessandro, was a man of his generation – quite stern but also intellectual. From him Maria would understand the "self-discipline necessary to overcome many of the obstacles she would have to face during her life."[68] Her long-time collaborator and protégé, Anna Maccheroni, provides additional insight into the young Montessori, writing about a seriously ill 10-year-old Maria telling her mother "Do not worry, mother, I cannot die; I have too much to do."[69]

Another story, shared by Montessori collaborator and biographer, E.M. Standing, concerns Montessori's challenges as the only woman in medical school. The animosity of the male students and the requirement that she had to be alone in the dissecting room took their toll. One day:

> . . . overwhelmed by the feeling of despair . . . she left the dissecting room with her mind quite made up to seek another career less strewn with obstacles. As she walked along she passed a shabbily dressed woman accompanied by a child of some two years of age. The woman began to beg. It was not the woman, however, but the child who was destined to alter the course of her life. Whilst the mother tuned up her professional whine, the young child, quite unconcerned continued to sit on the ground playing with a small piece of colored paper. There was something in the child's expression so serenely happy in the possession of that worthless scrap of colored paper, observing it with the full absorption of

its little soul – that, suddenly [Montessori] was moved by emotions she could not herself explain and turned around, and went back to the dissecting room. . . . In this we see an example of the mysterious affinity that exists deep down in the soul of the genius towards that work which [she] is destined to perform.[70]

When confronted with the most difficult situations, we are often tested, and our true power and value comes to the surface. Montessori would later reflect "It was almost as if I was keeping myself for an unknown mission."[71] Standing also shares:

I once heard [Montessori] expound on a theory that the art of life consists in learning how "to be obedient to events" . . . Rightly understood . . . this signifies a life full of generous acceptances of duties . . . leading to unexpected developments along the line of her genius . . . [resulting in] a series of experiences linking themselves to prepare for the next step.[72]

As I look back at all the influences and events in my own life, I can really relate to *a series of experiences linking themselves to prepare for the next step*. I think in all of our lives there are touchtone experiences that, if we listen to our heart, lead us further into the hero's journey or the journey of the self towards the Self. Montessori's early insights came as Inspiration for the revelations she would later uncover.

Another of those inspirational insights happened in 1906, a year before she opened the first *Casa dei Bambini*. During a lecture at the University of Rome she made two points: "The duty of the school, of the teacher, is to help, not to judge; and, mental work does not exhaust, it gives nourishment; it is food for our spirit."[73]

How did these two points arise in her consciousness? After graduating (1896) from medical school as one of the first female doctors in Italy, Montessori joined a research program at the University of Rome:

As part of her work at the clinic she would visit Rome's asylums for the insane, seeking patients for treatment. She relates how on one such visit, the caretaker of a children's asylum told her with disgust how the children grabbed crumbs from on the floor after their meal. Montessori realized that in such a bare, unfurnished room the children were desperate for sensorial stimulation and activities for their hands, and that this deprivation was contributing to their condition.[74]

Montessori wanted to learn more about the intellectually disabled[75] so she studied the work of Jean-Marc Itard and Eduard Séguin. Itard's groundbreaking research with the "Wild boy of Aveyron" provided Montessori with an insight into sensitive periods and planes of development – where learning is attuned to specific stages of growth for individuation and socialization.

Séguin followed in Itard's footsteps and developed an array of practical life and sensorial apparatus — experiences that would aid the intellectually challenged child. "Montessori was so keen to understand their work properly that she translated (hand-writing) all of it herself from French into Italian."[76] Education researcher, Katrina Myers, explains, "[Séguin] gave preference to real duties borrowed from daily use. The children thus trained are more practical, and so more helpful in their social relations."[77] Séguin developed an array of materials and he authored the three-period lesson.[78]

Between 1898 and 1900 Montessori embraced Séguin's approach, applying and improving upon his contributions. Her work received much attention, but she still wanted to study more, so she enrolled for a second degree at the University of Rome – in education, experimental psychology, and anthropology. Soon after, she was given a post as lecturer at the University of Rome's School of Education.

Throughout these early years there was an underlying question that permeated her thinking: *In what ways might ordinary children respond to the same educational methods employed with the intellectually disabled?* In 1907 she was given an opportunity to work with disadvantaged children at San Lorenzo,

Rome. This was the official beginning of the *Montessori Method*. From the outset of her work with the intellectually disabled, she believed the principles could be universally applied. Montessori explains:

> This feeling, so deep as to be in the nature of an intuition, became my controlling idea after I had left the school for [the intellectually disabled], and little by little, I became convinced that similar methods applied to [ordinary] children would develop or set their personality free in a marvelous and surprising way.[79]

Right from the beginning, Montessori knew her "method" was not a means to an end. It was a means in and of itself for releasing human potential. She did not want to educate teachers as mechanical practitioners. In his book, *Ends and Means*, Aldous Huxley contrasts Montessori teaching and learning in juxtaposition to the *ends* sought in traditional education that is training "for life in a hierarchical, militaristic society in which people are abjectly obedient to their superiors and inhuman to their inferiors."[80] In juxtaposition, Montessori says:

> It is my belief that what we should cultivate in our teachers is more the *spirit* than the mechanical skill of the scientists; that is, the *direction* of the *preparation* should be towards the spirit rather than toward the mechanism.[81]

In Montessori's time educators saw children as "not yet" – a vessel that had to be filled with knowledge and information. *She* knew the child as a spiritual being, declaring in 1909:

> There are some who claim the mistaken conviction that a child's natural education should be wholly physical; but the Spirit also has its nature, and it is the life of the spirit that should dominate human existence at every stage.[82]

Also by 1909, clear seeds of a vision that would expand throughout her life, culminating with profound experiences whilst living in India (1939-1946 and 1947-1949). She charges:

> We have been mistaken in thinking that the natural education of children should be purely physical; the soul, too, has its nature, which it is intended to perfect in the spiritual life: the dominating power of human existence throughout all time.[83]

Two years after opening the first Children's House she proclaimed, "In education we are now concerned with interest in the human race and culture, which is only one nation …the world."[84] Early on Montessori knew she had tapped into something extraordinary. She would spend the rest of her life exploring and expanding on this, naming the approach *Cosmic Education*.

Montessori begins to articulate these ideas during six Cosmic Education lectures in 1935-36, followed by other lectures during the late 1930s, and concluding with profound realizations during her stay in India (1939-1946, 1947-1949). When I first read those lectures, I was reminded of the words of Julian Huxley, older brother of Aldous Huxley. The elder Huxley's 1926 book, *The Stream of Life*, was one of Montessori's references. He proclaims, "Let us not forget that we [humans] are the trustees of evolution, and that the refusal to face this problem is to betray the trust put into our hands by the powers of the universe."[85]

From the very beginning, Maria Montessori approached her work with children not as a pedagogue who wanted to apply a methodology, but as a medical doctor who was rigorously trained in the scientific method. Her observations of those first children and the way they set about their purposeful work – work that required both physical and mental focus and attention – was as clinical as it was revelatory.

Through scientific observation she was a witness to nothing less than a miracle. Those emergent truths of normalization bear restating: *deep concentration, collaboration, bbiophilia, joy, love of work, love of repetition, empathy, humility as well as compassion, independence, cooperation, and love of silence.* She was deeply surprised by the qualities that the children presented in this first "prepared environment." She thought that it must be attributable to the Divine. Close collaborator and Montessori translator, Claude Claremont, writes:

> Throughout the whole of Dr. Montessori's lectures to her students
> there runs an endless refrain, the insistence and emphatic appeal to
> science. It is more than the substratum from which her work has
> sprung: it is the very substance of her creation itself, the material
> of which all her thought is woven.[86]

No matter where she went in the world, giving courses for teachers or public lecturers, she presented a grand and lofty vision for education and its potential to give humanity a universal view that would contribute to the common well-being. She had "discovered" a process that would liberate both learner and teacher in a co-transformative experience. Her universal ideas coalesced for decades and were meticulously shared under the title of "Cosmic Education" at the end of her 1935 International Course for teachers. Strongly influenced by geologist Antonio Stoppani (1824-1891), and through the lens of empirical science, Montessori methodically takes her audience of teachers through the geo-biological cycles of the Earth, explaining the significance of work-activity throughout the living world. These ideas were *not for her students to present to the children,* but for their own information as a way to grasp the essence of how the Earth behaves in an interdependent "cosmic" way.[87] During these lectures she points the way forward to scientific discoveries that had not yet been realized. Whilst explaining to her students how the Earth functions as a whole, she essentially describes:

(1) The Gaia Hypothesis

Montessori poses the question "Why is seawater maintained in a steady-state, at composition which allows living creatures to live?"[88] This is one of the principles of the not-yet articulated Gaia Hypothesis proposed by Lynn Margulis and Jim

Lovelock 30 years later. One of its tenets is that planetary-wide homeostasis allows the oceans to maintain 4% salinity.

And later, in *To Educate the Human Potential* she talks about the Earth as a living organism.

> We hear much talk . . . of world organization but the word that should rather be used is '*Organism*'. When it is recognized that the world is already a living organism, its vital functions may be less impeded in their operation, and it may consciously enter on its heritage.[89]

(2) Autopoiesis (Santiago Theory of Cognition)

Autopoiesis, proposed 40 years later by Humberto Maturana and Francisco Varela, is a new definition of life, where life has both the capacity for self-making whilst coupling to the environment to create novelty. Montessori intuits this by saying, "living beings create their own environment and form their own conditions of life."[90]

(3) Earth Systems Science

With her scientific mind, Montessori analyzes the cycles that not only distribute minerals to living beings, but also add to the creation of Earth itself. Her integration of geology, biology, and oceanography was 60 years ahead of the field that defines these cycles.

Montessori carefully follows the geo-biological cycle of calcium carbonate (limestone) and how it flows through the inorganic world by way of rivers that carry the substances from mountains and landmasses via erosion into the oceans. She identifies the work of shellfish and corals that absorb the calcium carbonate, not only to purify the water for other marine life, but also to use these substances so that "Life remakes the Earth."[91] They give back by purifying the water for other forms of sea life and by leaving their remains as matter that build land masses and mountains.

Why does Montessori painstakingly lecture about these finite details to her students? She even states that she hopes she is not "boring" them, that she is only trying to give an "example or pattern" that is relevant throughout creation. She tells them that she knows they would be more interested in listening to practical matters.[92]

These six lectures are not an easy read. Montessori did not use a script; she spoke from notes or extemporaneously. What we read today – even in her books (except for the earliest ones) – is the result of sentence by sentence translation of lectures, most probably by Claude Claremont (1930s) and her son, Mario (1940s) who spoke English with an Italian accent. This was the way I studied Montessori in Italy during 1973. The lectures were in Italian and we wrote feverishly as the translation was given in English, hoping there would be enough time to finish the writing while the next part was given in Italian. I learned all sorts of shorthand! The sentence structure of my notes reveals the sentence structure of translated Italian, which doesn't always sound accessible in English. But one can grok the ideas and get the perfume of their essence.[93]

With these lectures Montessori is driving towards a goal and that goal is to bring her students to the realization that life on Earth, each in its own unique manifestation, has a flow-through Cosmic Task – that when plants and animals satisfy their need for survival, they perform unconscious work that contributes to the well-being of the Earth's economy.[94] It is *work* itself, done unconsciously, that allows the Earth to sustain itself. Montessori explains:

> What we want to stress here is the importance of the activity of life in the Earth's [cycles]. Life contributes to everything; it inter-venes both in the formation of the Earth and in the equilibrium between its elements.[95]

And she continues, "We might call this the great wisdom of nature, knowing how to follow one's own laws, the laws that lead to harmony and universal obedience."[96]

But, she intervenes, humans are different. Whereas all other beings "give back" unconsciously, modern humans need experiences and understanding to comprehend the need to give back/contribute. For eons we, too, were integral to Earth flow-through; however, with our reflective consciousness and technological intelligence we have been able to transform nature. Montessori uses the prefix *supra* meaning "above" to designate the supra-nature that is created by supra-humans. *Above* does not infer better, only that humanity has supra-imposed a new, technological nature upon nature.[97] Today we would say, "*Yes, but look what we have done!*" And Montessori might reply, "*The right kind of education would assuage the negative influence humans are having on Earth's cycles. This would be an education leading towards normalization and contextualized by humanity's cosmic responsibility for giving back.*"

She also addressed her belief that humans have the ability to create a "new spiritual sphere above the world" rather than "being a bitter source of suffering"[98] It was not until 1950 that she named this the *psychosphere,* denoting the domain where "there is only one civilization" that represents the "unity of [human]kind."[99] This wisdom is reminiscent of the contributions of her scientific and philosophical contemporaries, Teilhard de Chardin, Eduard LeRoy, and Vladimir Vernadsky, all of whom proposed the existence of a *noosphere* – a sphere of human thought and consciousness above and beyond the biosphere.

The stability point for implementing the Montessori Method is *work-activity* and *appreciation-gratitude.* Without purposeful work, independently chosen by the child, deviations may occur in the human personality and supra-nature will be dominated by its own deceptive conditioning... that is, taking more than necessary whilst not giving back what is required for the flow of life.

She observed that the pathway to normalization follows the innate cosmic laws of *work,* which includes an awareness of the natural environment leading to appreciation and gratitude. In fact, and without question, humanity, creating its technological nature upon nature, does have the possibility to maintain the flow – the cycle of life throughout the Gaian economy – aligned with the laws of the cosmos. However, because humanity does not understand its impact, it often impedes the natural flow, thereby harming the Gaian flow-through.

———————◇———————

During the late 1930s George Arundale, head of the Theosophical Society, and his wife Rukmini Devi met with Montessori and invited her to come to India. Montessori, who had earlier connections with Mahatma Gandhi, was intrigued by the opportunity to go to someplace where poverty was rampant and where education was needed on a massive scale. There were already Montessori schools in India because students had come to her courses in the United Kingdom and gone back to India to teach, but these were mostly for the wealthy. Despite approaching her 70th birthday, she accepted the Arundales' invitation and left Europe in October, 1939 for lecturing and coursework. I know how challenging travel can be during one's eighth decade and I am impressed with her gumption and fortitude. Little did she know that the war would breakout, preventing her return to Europe for seven years.

MONTESSORI IN INDIA

I asked Vedic astrologer, Drupada MacDonald, what it might have been like for Maria Montessori coming to India for the first time in 1939. This is his response:

> As a western born person, who visits India often, I don't have to think too much about my answer. It is common in Indian culture not to just talk about God, but to talk to God. God is the nearest of the near and the dearest of the dear and lots of people have very real relationships with this Consciousness. Whether you call it Divine Mother, Heavenly Father, Krishna, Rama, Ganesh, Hanuman or the Infinite Light and/or Love, it is all of these and more. I am currently in Assisi (Italy) where one can still feel the energy that St. Francis awakened some 700 years ago. It is tangible. He was one saint with many followers that created a movement that touched this land, and society. That energy is still living.

In India, every place has had many many St. Francis-type beings over the last 4000 years. Who knows how many. Thousands? Millions? You can feel it in the "air" if you are sensitive. I would guess that Maria Montessori was filled with spiritual inspiration in India. I know that I sure have felt it when there.[100]

Other close friends who travel regularly to India say it is a heart-centered and story-telling culture where spirituality is not hidden. Knowing how Montessori appreciated metaphor and was skilled at using parables for emphasis when she was lecturing, I have a sense that she must have felt quite at home in the way Indians tell stories.

Living in the Theosophical compounds at Adyar and Kodaikanal during her time in India, I imagine Montessori waking up to the sound of chanting – beautiful Kirtan chanting. With roots in the Vedic tradition, a Kirtan is a call-and-response style song, expressing loving devotion and spiritual ideas. Even without understanding the words, the music itself stirs the soul.

Although she traveled throughout Europe and visited North and South America, Montessori had never lived close to nature for an extended period. Of course she had short periods of time in natural settings. Her grandson, Mario, Jr., told me that in the summers they would live on a farm in the eastern part of Germany. In fact, he explained that her ideas about Erdkinder were born observing her adolescent grandchildren *work* the farm. But India would be the first time she actually lived in a natural setting for a prolonged period. Walking and being in nature, she viscerally experienced the cosmic flow-through she talked about in 1935. I know that when I am in the nearby forest, my body and mind have a primal experience just noticing-observing and then dropping into awe and wonder, followed by how and why questions, and then back to awe and wonder.

Living in a totally different, non-Western, culture, I imagine Montessori must have gone through a period of physical and emotional adjustments. Yet she was also surrounded by beauty – exotic flora, gorgeous flowers, sweet fragrances, colorful saris, face painting… new encounters for a person with heightened sensitivities to life. Montessori's level of understanding, as documented by the lectures she gave and books published during the India years, demonstrates deeper and wider understanding and insight as well as implications for the future development of humankind.

In what ways was India such an extraordinary experience for Montessori? During those 1935-36 lectures on Cosmic Education the "cosmic" she referred to was Earth-based: one that demonstrates how all organic and inorganic entities are interconnected and interdependent. In India, she gained insight into how lessons might be developed for children over 6 years of age. At the same time, the framework for her contribution to humanity expanded, incorporating the idea of *cosmic consciousness*.

In *The Absorbent Mind* Montessori points to Western philosophers Henri Bergson and William James as sources of inspiration. One of their common explorations was the notion of cosmic consciousness. During the India years Montessori was hosted by the Theosophical Society and embedded in a Buddhist and Hindu culture. This gave her an opportunity to observe cosmic consciousness from an Eastern perspective. In *The Absorbent Mind* she refers to the Bhagavad Gita by saying:

> One is tempted to say that the children are performing spiritual exercises, having found the path of self-perfect(ing) and ascent to the inner heights of the soul. Their work, in its development, reminds one of the principles to be found in the Indian book of wisdom, the Gita.[101]

Chapter 11 of the Gita is titled, *The Cosmic Vision*, and Chapter 12, *The Way of Love*. From the beginning of her work with children a prevailing ethos was the importance of Love. As early as 1915, Montessori embraced love in the form of the child when she said, "We all know that we could not put love in the heart of humans if it were not there in nature. What is necessary is that the flame of love which exists be free to expand."[102] In India her view of Love expanded on a cosmic scale:

[Love] can be considered from the point of view of life itself. Then we see it not only as something imagined or desired, but also as the reality of an eternal energy that nothing can destroy . . . This force that we call love is the greatest energy of the universe . . . it is far more than energy: it is creation itself. . . . I should put it better if I were to say, "God is Love."[103]

Montessori continues:

. . . love is much more than we have said so far. . . . With us [Love] is nothing other than one aspect of a very complex universal force, that — denoted by the words "attraction" and "affinity" — rules the world, keeps the stars in their courses, causes the conjunction of atoms to form new substances and holds things down on the Earth's surface. It is the force that regulates and orders the organic and inorganic that becomes incorporated into the essence of everything . . . Like a guide to salvation and to the endlessness of evolution . . . it is generally unconscious, but in life it sometimes assumes consciousness, and when felt in the human heart we call it Love.[104]

And she ends *The Absorbent Mind* with, "Love is conceded to humans as a gift that is directed for a certain purpose and a special reason and, in that, it resembles everything lent to human beings by the cosmic consciousness."[105]

Immediately after citing the Bhagavad Gita, Montessori draws readers' attention to the words of Kahlil Gibran, "Work is love made visible," thus taking the reader back to her original 1907 epiphany about the nature of work and the normalizing process. She now adds that only "healthy occupations" will result in "Spiritual development."[106] *Work is Love made visible!* I can imagine Montessori's response when she first read those words.[107]

From the very beginning she knew that when children are engaged in meaningful activity/work as well as authentic relationships with nature, they not only learn the how, what, and why, but they also develop personality attributes like appreciation, gratitude, and empathy. There is also a dynamic anticipation – an attraction of sorts – to the work itself. This has been my personal experience while working with children and adults.

Led by intuition, insight, inspiration and the science of observation, Montessori created learning environments for children that met their physical, social, intellectual, and spiritual needs. How did she do this? By generating opportunities for young people to sensorially learn about their culture and the natural world through activity and contemplation. For the child between the ages of 2 ½ and 6 that work/activity is the gateway into the normalizing process I have previously explored.

During those 1935-36 lectures Montessori methodically shows that every living being on Earth performs work to satisfy its needs. She urges her audience to recall that from the very beginning at San Lorenzo, her intuition about the child's need for work was *truth itself revealed*. In India she discovered the next level of *work* to engage the child after 6 years of age.

How might one create a learning environment that extends the inner development of the earlier years? Since the capacity of the imagination is in full blossom, might this be a time to invite children into an exploration of the Universe and cosmic consciousness itself? What experiences might enable them to be in awe of their inheritance and realize that each human being has a responsibility to contribute, to give back?

In order to strike the imagination of the learner to explore culture and science, the teacher of the elementary age child is a good storyteller – a Renaissance person with a passion for learning that crosses all disciplines. This teacher knows the art of asking the right question at the right time. Montessori explains:

> Since it is necessary to give so much to the children, let us give them a vision of the whole universe. The universe is an imposing reality and the answer to all questions. We shall walk together on this path of life. All things are part of the universe and are connected with each other to form one whole unity.[108]

And she continues:

> If the idea of the universe be presented to the children in the
> right way, it will do more than just arouse their interest, it will
> create in them admiration and wonder. ... The child's mind will
> no longer wander but becomes fixed and can *work*. The knowl-
> edge ... acquired is organized and systematic; their intelligence
> becomes whole and complete because the vision of the whole
> has been presented and their interest spreads, for everything is
> linked and has its place in the universe on which their minds are
> centered. The stars, the earth, the stones, life of all kinds form a
> whole in relation to each other and so close is this relation that
> we cannot understand a stone without some understanding of
> the great sun! No matter what we touch, an atom, or a cell, we
> cannot explain it without knowledge of the wider universe. What
> better answer can be given to those who quest for knowledge? .
> . . *How did the universe come into being and how will it end? . . .*
> *What am I? What is the task of humans in this wonderful universe?*
> *Do we merely live here for ourselves or is there something more for us*
> *to do?*[109] (Author's emphasis.)

In a recent cosmic story presentation about bacteria and blue-green algae given
to children at Nova Montessori School in Christchurch, New Zealand, one
6-year old girl, Georgie, had a very personal experience. As the guide, Pauline
Matsis, describes the event, she asked the children "What might be the giving
back of the bacteria, of the blue green algae; and, what might be the giving
back of each of you?"

Later that day, six-year old Georgie visited her in the office. She had
drawn a picture of bacteria, and in her own words, and from her own heart,
had responded to the moral of the story with these words:

> A lot of Bacterea is good. But some Bacterea is harmful. But with-
> out Bacterea we would not be here. Bacterea made us become on

erth. Bacterea is very very clever. And it is allso very very small. We can not see it without a Micrescop. An bacterea is very very intresting. I like Bacterea. It is so intresting. I like haw Bacterea got us on erth. I like Bacterea so much.

Pauline asked her why she found bacteria so interesting. As transcribed by Pauline, this was Georgie's reply:

They did so much for everything and everybody and every animal and nothing would be here without them. The blue green algae were so special that it gave the Earth oxygen and this made the atmosphere very special. It helped everything to breathe and the plants could live as well as the animals.

Bacteria helped me to know what I needed to do and that I will give back to all the people and the animals and to everything on the Earth. If the algae had not been here and did not give back, I would not be here and my mummy and daddy would not be here and all my friends ....and EVERYTHING!

I want to give back to Earth and I will give back kindness and love. That does not mean to just say love words, but to do love things. Like be kind to animals, and I want to find what I am giving back and I think that is love.

———————◇———————

During 1942, with the war expanding to Asian soil, Montessori shifted from Adyar in the north to the Kodaikanal hill country of southern India. Christina Trudeau, author of *Montessori's Years in India*, interviewed Lena Wikramaratne about Montessori's time at Kodaikanal, and came to the conclusion that the "setting of Montessori's living arrangements" could be called "mystical."[110] Trudeau continues, ". . .the beauty of the Kodaikanal hills, dotted with eucalyptus and pine trees to protect a lake, streams, foliage and an abundance of natural life . . . was an environment conducive to cosmic ideas."[111]

Without the didactic apparatus that they could not acquire from Europe because of the war, the outside – nature – became the primary learning environment. Accompanying Mario into that natural world was Lena Wikramaratne, who had been following Montessori's courses since the first one at Adyar. They worked with the children outside and then would share their findings with Maria Montessori. Mario Montessori, Sr. says "We saw purpose in everything that existed: nature's equilibrium was maintained. The rain – why did it rain here and not there – the atmosphere, the sun; each had its role to play."[112] The children received lessons in response to their observations. To understand more deeply, the teachers and children would take what they had observed and learned in nature and create materials – charts, nomenclature – that explored the biological and geological discoveries they encountered.

The Cosmic Education lectures came to life in the gardens of their outdoor "classroom" with lessons to satiate the older child's vast interest to know everything. Throughout *To Educate the Human Potential*, Montessori describes the content of *contextual* stories that children between 6 and 12 years could be presented. (I am not quite sure when these stories were actually given to the children in a way that strikes their imagination. It may have been in India or even developed by Mario and others after Maria Montessori's death.) These stories plant seeds for even further exploration to answer "big" questions – all set into motion by a flaming desire to understand how nature works. This is the generative question: *In what ways does nature show us how the biological need to contribute is a comprehensive context throughout the natural world?* In order for the Earth to be self-sustaining, every entity has a Cosmic Task to "give back." Now the follow-on questions are: *What is humanity's Cosmic Task? What is your Cosmic Task?*

Many Montessori teachers begin with the Story of the Universe to provide the overarching context. However, in India the explorations began in nature, in a garden. Why not begin with the concrete – Gaia – and create a sense of wonder around a forest niche – or seaside, or mountain, or a garden, or any place in nature? The adult poses exploratory questions. In the silence of the space, s/he says: *What do you notice? What do you smell? What do you hear? What are the interconnections – Earth's natural systems – that maintain these patterns? How did all this come to be?*

After some time, the teacher ponders with the children:

Perhaps the cosmos has a story to tell us about how all of this came into being. It is a story about stars and supernovae, solar systems and planets, bacteria, humans, and polar bears. Would you like to hear more?

"Everything you see right now, right here, and everywhere, was born when our grandmother star exploded a very, very long time ago. Shall I continue?"

Based on the work with older children at Kodaikanal, Montessori observed and experienced the possibility of a new consciousness, a cosmic consciousness, emerging when children are given an opportunity to realize nature's interdependence simultaneously with sharing contextual stories about the Universe, the functioning of the Earth and the coming of life and humans.[113] These stories enable children to experience – through their imagination – an interconnected Universe, from the most expansive grandeur of the cosmos to the microcosm of single cell beings. All the stories embrace the ubiquitous imperative of "giving back." One could say that cosmic consciousness makes Indra's Net visible.

I think Montessori would have deeply enjoyed the 3000-year-old Indra's Net story and parable, which is found in both Hindu and Buddhist traditions. There is no evidence that she had direct knowledge, but even if she didn't, it would have been in the Indian air, so to speak.

In the house of Indra there is said to be a network of crystal beads so arranged that if you look at one you will see all the others reflected in it. In the same way, each object in the world is not merely itself but involves every other object, and in fact, is every other object.

There is an endless net of threads throughout the universe.
The horizontal threads are in space;

the vertical threads in time.
At every crossing of threads there is an individual,
and every individual is a crystal bead.
The Great Light of Absolute Being illuminates
and penetrates every crystal bead.
And also, every crystal bead reflects not only the light
from every other crystal in the net,
But also every reflection of every reflection throughout the universe.[114]

Montessori's insight into Cosmic Education reflects the essence of this verse. I feel it in these words, shared during my Montessori studies at Bergamo:

Each expression of everything that exists has a cosmic sense, and the union of these cosmic finalities not only maintains the level of existence, but increases it. Each being answers a special call that is beyond comprehension but which renders everything a participant in creation. All creatures consciously work for themselves, but the real aim of life is the absolute and unconscious obedience to the great laws that govern the universe. All the powers working in the cosmos have a special role. Physical powers, chemical powers and vital powers, all unconsciously collaborate in this great cosmic work.[115]

In India Montessori fully realized the potential her ideas had for the transformation of humanity. The books cited below were transcribed from her Indian courses and public lectures.

Reconstruction in Education (1942)

"This is the hope we have – a hope in a new humanity that will come from this new education, an education that is a collaboration of human and the universe, that is, a help for the incarnation of humanity."[116]

Education for a New World (1946)[117]

When following the Montessori Method "...teachers will witness the unfolding of the human soul and the rising of a New Human who will not be a victim of events but will have the clarity of vision to direct and shape the future of human society."[118]

Formation of Man (1955 –India lectures given during the 1940s)

In this work Montessori addresses the need to provide a "cosmic vision of history and the evolution of life,"[119] explaining that a "universal revolution is what we need . . . where cooperation of consciousness is necessary."[120] And she concedes "what is called the Montessori Method revolves . . . around the process of normalization within the labyrinth of the soul."[121]

Both Hindu and Buddhist traditions embrace the interdependence of all things: Oneness within the Universe, Divine or cosmic order, and human compassion. "The core of Theosophy was the Indian doctrines of the union of the human soul with divine consciousness."[122] Theosophy had its roots with an understanding of cosmogenesis, which deals with the origin and evolution of the Universe. Adyar was the worldwide center for these teachings.

In a 1946 lecture on Cosmic Education, Montessori expresses the "power of humanity as a cosmic agent." And then infers that ideas like this "were felt by intuition in the religions of thousands of years ago, identifying "a series of very ancient writings . . . collected in a book called the Ahinahita, which showed the human path to reach God." She cites a passage in the Ahinahita "to redeem the earth and to transform the deserts into Paradise." It seems that her years in India affirmed her own belief system as she spells out, "It is through this work . . . that humanity will grow to the point of approaching the understanding of God."[123]

Indian spiritual teacher, Sri Chinmoy expresses a similar notion when he says, "The aim of life is to be the conscious expression of the Eternal Being...

Each life is a microcosm. Whatever breathes in the vast universe also breathes in each individual life."[124]

The perennial philosophy is a perspective that views all of the world's religious traditions as sharing a metaphysical truth or origin from which all esoteric and exoteric knowledge and doctrine has grown.[125] Already cited in Chapter Six, according to Huxley that wisdom can be defined by three truth statements:

1. There is an infinite, changeless reality beneath the world of change.
2. This same reality lies at the very core of every human personality.
3. The purpose of life is to discover this reality experientially: that is, to realize God while here on Earth.

For Montessori "the infinite changeless reality beneath the world of change" is that each being across creation, in the process of meeting its own needs for survival, automatically gives back, contributes to creation, and maintains the cosmic order. Although Montessori would agree with the assertion, "this same reality lies at the very core of every human personality," she would say that with humanity there has to be a form of education – Cosmic Education – wherein one establishes a fertile ground for the expression of this reality... activities that embrace humanity's Cosmic Task. As for "realizing God while here on Earth," in the book, *Education and Peace*, Montessori says:

> Like a radio set that can receive the long and short waves that are transmitted through space, the sort of instrument children construct in their own souls is destined to receive the holy waves transmitting divine love through the boundless spheres of eternity. . . . humans . . . can receive the emanations of the Godhead.[126]

And in her final 1946 Indian lecture on Cosmic Education, right before returning to Europe, she says, "The secret of education is to recognize and observe the divine in humanity: that is, to know, love and serve the divine in humanity." Underlying the cosmic lessons is the message "Obey God and become like God."[127]

I have explored Montessori's path of inner wisdom, from its beginnings in her childhood, to becoming a doctor, and then entering into education, not as a pedagogue, but as someone who saw the possibility for liberating the soul of the child to walk in alignment with Divine Goodness. Her lifetime reveals a personal and collective potential for humanity to transcend dogma in communion with Universal oneness, the Divine within.

I believe Maria Montessori's years in India gave these ideas an opportunity to express themselves. The pendulum had already swung in this direction before India, not arrived at theoretically or through intellectual filtering, but directly through observation of children. She observed the necessity for activity-work in order for children to grow towards independence. It was not any work, but a particular organization of activity that satisfied their inner need to be in relationship with the natural world as well as become competent members of the culture. That this would lead to deep concentration, compassion, and congruence between inner and outer personality was a discovery that unfolded rather spontaneously.

What happened in India was a continuation and exclamation point to what she had studied with her science and intuited with an awakening consciousness. The science was solid. She knew about geo-biological cycles – and the role of life as an integral homeostatic presence. Her work with children under 6 years of age revealed that when they are exposed to purposeful activity they would not only engage the culture, but as previously noted, would also develop personality characteristics that were in harmony with life. With this as a foundation, nothing less than a grand cosmic immersion could be undertaken for children over the age of 6 – one based on experiences in nature and stories about the cosmos. Cosmic Education actually begins with the very young children as they are introduced to gardening and the natural world and take in the essence of flower, tree, rain, and wind. When our grandson, Max, was three years old, he came to Marsha to say he was hungry. Marsha replied, "Would you like to eat the sunlight?" He looked puzzled. They went outside where Max picked an orange off the tree, and Marsha offered segments that looked like slices of the sun. "You are eating the sunlight that helped create the orange." An hour later, Max appeared and asked if he could eat some more sunlight: this time, an apple.

Cosmic Education extends into adolescence as a time to go deeply into Earth systems science –the integration of ecology and cosmology– to study the details of what they experienced through listening and participating in stories during the previous years. Adolescents need to understand the significance of being human and the contributions that each person has the capacity to make. They have a desire to contribute and make a difference; it is a time for them to expand their commitment to their community – a period of life for meaningful "giving back" experiences. One might say that Cosmic Education for adolescence is an invitation into the sacred life of the culture.

The years in India provided Montessori with a synthesis of how to present these ideas to young people. It also provided her with opportunities to live and work in a deeply spiritual culture embedded in a deeply spiritual natural environment. In the widest possible sense, these years were a gestation period where she integrated the singularity of Heaven and Earth, Cosmos and Gaia. India provided fertile soil on which to grow her relationship with the Godhead. The Indian and Theosophical culture was not the singular source of these ideas, for they had been emerging throughout Montessori's life, but that milieu did provide a nesting space for this wisdom to flourish.

The Montessori way, as seen in Figure 6, begins at birth and continues throughout life for it is no less than the soul's journey of the self toward the Self.

It is educating for right-action and love.

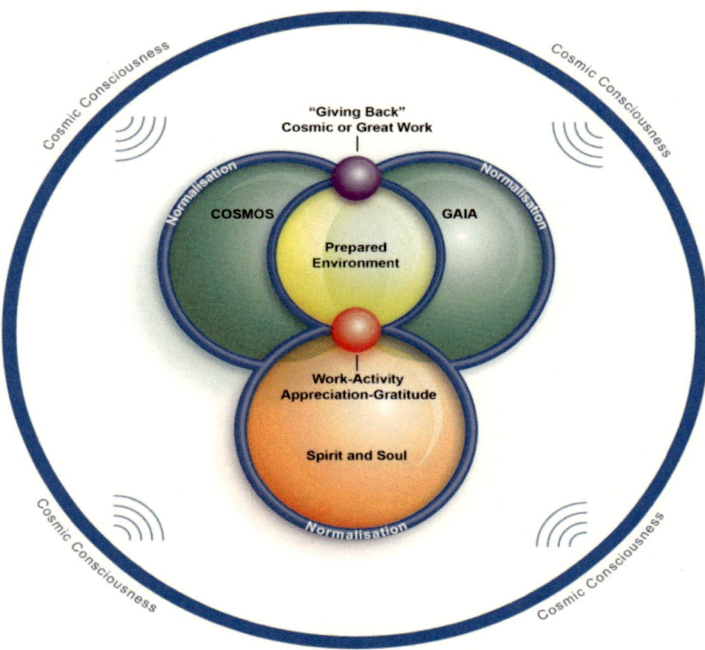

Figure 6. Natural Map of Montessori Essence

CHAPTER TEN:
TO EDUCATE ECO-SAPIENS[128]

Eco from the Greek oikos, "house," referring to Cosmos as our house-home.
Sapiens from the Latin sapere, "to be wise."

(Voice of Gaia)

I am Gaia. I represent the entire Earth community, which includes all beings
– humans, animals, plants and all forms that enable me to manifest my innate
wisdom. I maintain processes for Earth's dynamic balance. What you do to the
Earth, you do to that dynamic balance. If you are kind, gentle, and respectful to
Gaia, you are kind, gentle, and respectful to yourself.

I am not an abstraction. I am you and you are me.

Deep-seated, deep-rooted connections
Opening the portals to wider awareness
Embracing the cosmic dance of
Differentiation
Autopoiesis
and Communion

Well into my eighth decade on planet Earth, I have found a home that resonates with my heart, mind, and soul. When I go for walks I sometimes feel
like I am in a wilderness area away from dense populations, but in reality I am

in a heavily wooded area within the city limits of Portland, Oregon, with its many forested parks and endless trails where nature touches my soul. I live in a rain forest. Why is that important? How do I feel when I am embedded in nature? It changes everything. I hear the trees whispering, "Welcome home." I feel connected to Earth's rhythmic pulse. Awareness freezes past and future. There is communion.

Deep in the body forest
I give my breath to the natural totems
I give my senses to observing
the expressions of Earth.

After some minutes being present in this sensorial world, thought subsides and something emerges from deep within that expresses the what-is of now… truth, inspiration. The trees share their wisdom. There is a dialogue. They inspire me and remind me of the journey. I pose questions and listen carefully to responses. Embedding myself in Gaia allows Spirit to sound its note to be aware and embrace the infinite wisdom.

My story
is your story
is the Universe story
is the Earth's story
is the Universe story.
My story
is your story.

I share my story with you, as this book is what it is because I am who I am. Our stories illuminate each other's lives. They open hearts to feel and eyes to see. Stories are our very nature. Joseph Campbell says that throughout millennia, humans from diverse regions of the world reveal story in mythical form, "pointing to a constant requirement in the human psyche for a centering, in terms of deep principles."[129] He describes the 1969 image of the Earth – looking back from the moon – as the mythical symbol of our time.

Since the dawn of human communication, we have shared our stories of deep time and mystery. Deep time is that sense of feeling-knowing, the invisible thread of connection to origin. The myths of indigenous peoples characteristically describe the creation, responding to the human need for a sense of place and time, a sense of belonging. Indigenous cultures tell deep time stories. Ed Edmo, a Shoshone-Bannock poet and traditional storyteller about Pacific Northwest's tribal culture, writes:

Grandfather,
storyteller,
I come to you with thirsty ears.

Grandfather,
storyteller,
weaving words of ancient strength,
words colored with ageless time,
words that are carried on the welcome wind,
words floating on rivers of purity.

Grandfather,
storyteller,
I come to hear wisdom;
wisdom that is not yours alone,
wisdom that you share;
wisdom I shall pass to the children.[130]

They tell stories to pass on their heritage and provide metaphors for the safekeeping of Gaia's dynamic balance. The continuation of their group depends on these stories. It is a primal dependence that those of us who live in the industrial world do not regularly experience. Separated from organic life-systems, ecological balance is an abstraction read about in books or heard in lectures.

Formalized schooling has been civilization's response to sharing knowledge with the rising generation. It accomplishes this through a 19th century mechanistic paradigm, parceling information in fixed categories called "subjects" and assigning grades based on how well the learner has memorized facts. Rewards and punishments are stimuli for meeting standards. What is the result? Competition, where ends trump means. The primary objective is to fill the empty vessel with information-knowledge for the function of getting a job and fitting in to the culture. Parents, concerned about their children's future, add their own fears about success, resulting in an exacerbation of conditioning by home and school.

So, where do young people engage the meaning of life? Who raises the exploratory questions for understanding of self and self in the world? The renowned spiritual teacher Jiddu Krishnamurti spent his life exploring the domain of psychological freedom. There is an ancestral and cultural imprint that prejudices, or conditions the mind, resulting in unexamined assumptions about life. He asserts that to rid oneself of these assumptions is freedom's gateway and the essential task of education. He names the process *unconditioning*. Krishnamurti explains:

> You are conditioned and the student is conditioned; your child
> is conditioned and the teacher, the educator is conditioned . . .
> In the school the teacher and the student are both conditioned.
> For the teacher to wait until he is unconditioned, he might just
> as well wait for the rest of his life. So the question is whether he
> and the student in their relationship in a school can uncondition
> themselves?[131]

Exploratory questions are essential. These are questions "worth thinking about" and take a different direction based on the developmental stage of the learner. Stories provide a sense of wonder and appreciation for the significance of life. They offer questions and metaphors to comprehend the mystery, and they identify the overarching contexts that shape who we are. They are an essential container in the unconditioning process.

I was fascinated by deep time by the age of 10, and recently, based on my work with children and adults for nearly 50 years, I created a series of contextual stories that include: "The Epoch of the First Nine Billion Years," "The Story of Earth," "The Coming of Life," and "The Human Story." These stories embrace the creativity in the Universe. The lens of exploration is the universal tendencies that exist through all space and all time: *Differentiation, autopoiesis, and communion.*

Autopoiesis, as described in Francesco Varela and Humberto Maturana's Santiago Theory, is a process of cognition. When a living being connects with its environment, learning takes place. All life, from single cell organisms to multicellular mammalian beings, is constantly in a cognitive process. Life is cognition. Life is learning. And learning is life. I find that profound.

Swimme explains:

> Differentiation was the first law that scientists could regard as universal among life and the Universe. It is amazing. At one time we were all hydrogen and helium gas. And then right away it starts differentiating into stars, each one different from the other, and then planetary systems come into being. So this movement to differentiation is very deep in the Universe.

Swimme takes Varela and Maturana's theory of autopoiesis and applies it to living entities and relates it to the macrocosm. He says:

> Recently another tendency has been observed and is identified as autopoiesis or self-organization. No one tells a cloud of hydrogen gas how to construct a galaxy; it is just in the nature of the Universe.

> For the third tendency, we say "communion," but interconnectivity would be another descriptor. It is the way in which the Universe becomes more progressively related. You start off with hydrogen gas, then after a while you have a planet, where there is an atmosphere moving into the hydrosphere. It is all interpenetrating. Then you have the development of life itself and eco-systems.[132]

As each contextual story unfolds, storytellers can be quite poetic in how they metaphorically introduce/imbue these concepts. Maria Montessori identifies the ages between 5-6 and 12 years as the sensitive period for story. She says:

> Our aim . . . is not merely to make the child understand, and still less to force him to memorise, but so to touch the imagination as to enthuse children to their inmost core.[133]

> . . . we must not begin by giving them elementary facts, . . . to make them merely understand its mechanism, but start with far loftier notions of a philosophical nature, put in an acceptable manner, suited to the child's psychology.[134]

And she extols an underlying theme that provides aspiration for the wisdom and the power to serve others. "All creatures work consciously for themselves, but the real purpose of their existence remains unconscious, yet claiming obedience [to universal tendencies]."[135]

As we have seen all along, Montessori calls this process Cosmic Education. It provides us with the capacity to fall into bliss with existence; to marvel at creativity; to observe the natural cycles; and, to be aware of being aware. It is significantly more than materials and lessons; it is a way into the spiritual essence of life. It is the foundation for right-action in each of our lives, embracing what Montessori identifies as the "unconscious love" throughout space and time.

Before the age of 5 or 6, the "preparation" for story is direct contact with the natural world – to observe, to use all the senses to absorb beauty, color, shape, and sound. Exploring the whole of the flower, the tree, the animal is more important than understanding the name or the name of its parts. The adult has to be ever so careful to help the young child grok rather than dissect. In this way children can appreciate the integrity of beingness.

As seen in Chapter Nine, the natural world is also the immersion point for older children to begin to connect with the finite and imagine the infinite. Through exploratory, reflective questions the 6 to 12 year old begins to comprehend the unity within the diversity expressed by Cosmos and Gaia. Reflective questioning is integral to Krishnamurti's notion of unconditioning. These questions allow for teacher and learner to explore issues from many perspectives. Reflection is essential and without judgment. *I wonder why?* and *I wonder how?* may be the arrows that deconstruct prejudices and assumptions.

For the learner beyond 12 years, the same stories are integral. Now, with an expanding self-reflective awareness, personal and group ritual, including the *Council of All Beings*, can make the implicit explicit.[136] Noting that the Universe is always pressing for further differentiation, autopoiesis, and communion provides young people an opportunity to explore how these scientific phenomena present themselves through stories.

———◇———

I am back in the forest surrounded by red cedar, fir, ash, and maple. With all the other life forms, I am inside a living, breathing diorama. I observe differentiation. How did all this diversity emerge? The Earth is alive and I gasp at the wonder of it all. I observe autopoiesis, self-replication in nature's offspring. This self-replication is dependent on interacting-coupling with the environment. Life needs nutrients from the environment in order to reproduce itself. And communion is omnipresent. I am embedded in an ecological community, an ecosystem where wholes and parts dance together to fulfill their Cosmic Tasks. And I am part of that niche – inhaling and exhaling – I give and I take.

When it comes to "The Human Story," for adolescents, engagement with mythology and heroes of the ancient world can also be explored through the lens of modern films like *Star Wars* and *The Matrix*. This leads to the work of Joseph Campbell and the *Power of Myth* and its relevance to what he names the "hero's journey." As shared earlier Campbell identifies three elements on the journey of re-inventing oneself: *separation, initiation, and return*. The keynote for the hero's journey is to follow one's bliss – listening to one's heart and pursuing truth.

Following one's bliss is the pathway to what Thomas Berry identifies as the *Great Work* and Maria Montessori calls our *Cosmic Task*. Ultimately, we live a life aligned with our values that will benefit the larger web of being – the ecosystem. To enter into one's Cosmic Task or Great Work, one has to deeply explore one's own story; stories that include challenging nodules need to be released or transformed in order to enter into a leadership capacity to carry one's vision forward. Otherwise there is a disconnect between who we are and what we do.

To embark on the hero's journey, a person observes a dissonance between self and the present reality. The call to adventure comes from a deep-rooted place of passion – a passion so strong that going forward becomes what Krishnamurti calls *choiceless awareness* – you see with complete attention, and there is an immediate knowing that may go beyond ordinary societal expectations. Thirteenth century mystical poet, Rumi says:

> *You are not a drop in the ocean.*
> *You are the entire ocean in a drop.*
>
> *Seek the wisdom that will untie your knot.*
> *Seek the path that demands your whole being.*[137]

As I look back on my life, I have experienced several periods of reinventing myself. On at least three occasions, mammoth changes have been undertaken where I have entered into the cycle of separation, initiation, and return.

After studying philosophy and psychology, as well as learning about Montessori education from a parent's perspective while befriending several teachers, I uprooted my entire family to go to Bergamo, Italy, for the Montessori teacher preparation course. I went through a yearlong initiation process and returned from Italy to work with children and adults to share what I had learned.

Feeling disassociated from Montessori organizations, including schools, in 1988, I removed myself from the preparation of teacher trainers' apprenticeship process, as well my position as head of school. I was searching for congruence between the Montessori method and the way Montessori organizations behaved, which included a way to prepare teachers in a process that was confluent with the process of working with young people.

As Joseph Campbell explains:

Follow your bliss
and the Universe will open doors
where there were only walls.[138]

In 1990 I was instrumental in the founding of the Global Alliance for Transforming Education (GATE) – a worldwide network of holistic education organizations. We published *Education 2000: A Holistic Perspective* (see Appendix II). Subsequently, I met and have worked with many renowned global leaders and 21st century visionaries. A six-year cycle of initiation into a new way of being in the world, including a three-year experience as faculty mentor at California Institute of Integral Studies (CIIS) – one of the first online doctoral programs, culminated with the creation of the TIES graduate programs in Integrative and Montessori Integrative Learning. This marked my "return" – implementing what I learned over that six-year span.

During this same stormy and creative period, I left a marriage of 30 years. I subsequently discovered profound love with Marsha Morgan, with whom I worked in concert for the next 20 years.

When Marsha began sinking into Alzheimer's, my world was turned upside down – again. This time "separation from the known" was forced upon me, and I began searching for new ground. A period of immense creativity followed her entrance into full-time care. It was, and still is, a search to understand at the deepest levels what we had created together and where I am taking it without her physical presence. Now, years later, I am in the process of articulating our discoveries.

These journeys of self-discovery are not limited to group or class; they are an integral part of the primordial archetype that resides in all of us – a seed in our consciousness that sprouts, and then doors open for the unfolding of story. Since this kernel is within every human, I began searching for similar patterns of cyclical development in meta-systemic organization. I did not have to look very far to answer the question: Might Joseph Campbell's journey of separation, initiation, and return be a further articulation of differentiation, autopoiesis, and communion?

Differentiation is the tendency towards new forms, new combinations, and complexification. Separation is the urgency to renew one's self when we feel separated from the current reality that surrounds us. Separation, then, is differentiation at a psychological level.

In autopoiesis, entities are continually self-making, both self-contained and in relationship (coupled) to their environment. Life needs, and is dependent upon, its environment for sustenance. And in the networking process, both life and its environment are transformed. In this way, the entire network continually "makes itself" while simultaneously bringing forth a world. During Campbell's initiation phase, we go through a process of gaining new wisdom-knowledge, creating a new self by going through structurally coupling – an initiation to step into our new identity.

Communion is the synergy that fosters more progressive relatedness. It results in integration, new networks, and increased adaptability. The outcome brings forth solar systems, planets, and ecosystems. In Campbell's notion of return, we come back to tell the story after initiation. This is a catalyst for others to embark on the re-creation pathway, expanding the network for new thinking-being.

During the 1970s, Jim Lovelock and Lynn Margulis collaborated on the Gaia Hypothesis, after the Greek goddess Mother Earth. Initially called a hypothesis, it has now been elevated to the status of Gaia Theory as we discover more and more about how the Earth's systems and cycles work collaboratively, replicating life from the micro to the macro level. The Earth, Gaia, is a living system of systems, appropriately called Mother Earth. Most native traditions resonate with this idea. They hear Gaia's voice and listen closely.

Ed McGaa, Eagle Man, is a member of the Lakota Sioux. He writes:

It is true that many of the old ways have been lost. But just as the life-giving rains restore the earth after the drought, so your power will restore the Way and give it new life.

We ask this not only for the red people but for all the people that may live. In ignorance and carelessness they have walked upon Ina Maka, Mother Earth. They did not understand that they are part of all beings, the four-legged, the winged, grandfather rock, the tree people, and our star brothers. Now the Earth and all our relations are crying out. They cry for the help of all people.[139]

What if we were all able to tune into Mother Earth, *Ina Maka*, Gaia? What might she tell us about her present situation?

Voice of Gaia

Please listen to me. Balancing my systems has always been a challenge, requiring extraordinary levels of cooperation. Over the eons, despite the sun's increased temperatures, the Earth's temperature has maintained its habitable zone, and I have been able to keep oxygen in the atmosphere in perfect balance; despite the continuous erosion of rocks containing high amounts of salt, I have been able to keep the salinity in the oceans in perfect balance. For over 3 billion years, I have been able to balance just about everything in all natural systems on which my life depends. However, during the last 200 years, with the increased presence of two-legged beings, many of my ecosystems that keep me alive are being destroyed. You who listen closely know what to do. You have the technology. Please help me on our journey. Find your innate wisdom for right-action.

Perhaps Gaia, acknowledging the impending peril, is organizing at levels we humans cannot perceive. Is it possible that Gaia needs us as much as we need Gaia? When we change, Gaia changes; when our consciousness expands, so does Gaia's in the ultimate structural coupling.

Each of us knows groups and individuals who have that innate wisdom for right-action. All one has to do is Google terms like ecological awareness, environmental science, Cosmic Education, planetary collective, Eco-sapiens, integrative learning, transformative learning, systems thinking, spirituality in education – the list could fill a book. You will discover people and organizations that have a vision for a different Earth community – one that lives in balance with each other and with the Earth.

Initiatives for the Earth's renewal are surfacing around the world. Might Gaia be entering the stage of recreating herself? Shifting from the current reality to one that takes her forward to living sustainably? What sort of initiation might be engaged to make the separation from the Gaia of now to the Gaia of tomorrow?

While working with the indigenous peoples of the Amazon, filmmaker Neal Rogin asked how the Pachamama Alliance might help. Their reply was simple, "Tell the story of everything to everyone." The result is the documentary *The Awakening Universe*. Films like this are very powerful and extremely important because they viscerally connect today with the 13.8 billion year story of our ancestors. Everything started with hydrogen and helium and now we have trees, giraffes, and opera singers.

My core question, the one that precipitated this book, the one that bears repeating, and heeds the advice "to tell the story of everything" is:

> *What are the contexts and processes in education that might liberate teachers and learners so that they* become *catalysts for a new human – one whose integral relationship with Gaia is bound by right-action and love?*

And the follow-on question might be:

> *How might dialogue and* exploratory *questions help build a sense of ecogenesis and cosmogenesis?*

In my 1989 book, *Rethinking Education*[140] I developed a view of humanity and nature that follows along significant paradigm shifts in human thinking about and interaction with Gaia. I define these stages (shown in Figure 7) as:

Humanity-in-Nature

Humanity-with-Nature

Humanity-over-Nature

Humanity-through-Nature

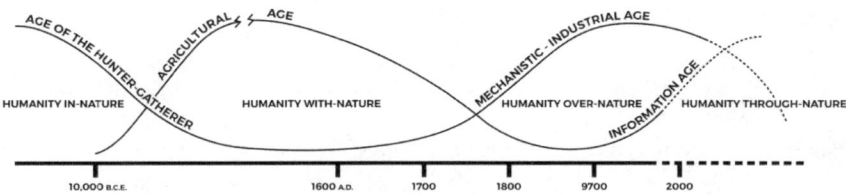

Figure 7. Human Paradigm Shifts. [From Gang, P. (1988)
Rethinking Education. Dagaz Press]

With humanity-in-nature, there is no differentiation between the "in here" and the "out there." We see this in their 30,000-year-old cave paintings. We see a texture of immersion in all worlds. They became the bison; they are the tree – in different states, in different forms. They were not "drawing" – spirit was drawing through them. Immersed in the natural world, they grasped meaning through connection and dependence, not scientifically, but viscerally.

In *Rethinking Education,* I wrote:

Humanity-through-nature is a giant shift in consciousness . . . It requires individuals to see the whole picture and is transformative. It is intuitive – beyond the mind . . . It is all things that Eastern philosophers and mystics knew about consciousness. As humanity-through-nature, the people of the 21st century have several responsibilities. We need to live by conscious choice and design within the ecological and resource limits of the planet. We need to develop effective alternatives to our current patterns of violence, particularly war. And we need a new orientation for our social, educational, and political institutions.[141]

Without any intention to develop that idea further at the time, I now see these past 30 years as my continued exploration of *humanity-through-nature* in education… to *see* with the awareness of humanity-in-nature, only now from the perspective of knowing that we are ecogenesis and cosmogenesis unfolding itself. Those contexts – ecogenesis and cosmogenesis – respond to the driving question of this book.

———◇———

I sit in alignment two meters from a huge Oregon red cedar. It is different from the rest of cedar trees and still different from all other trees, just as I am unique among all humans and humanity is unique amongst all other life forms. Uniqueness continues through larger and larger nested hierarchies – on Earth, amongst the planets in our solar system, within the Milky Way galaxy, and amongst all galaxies in the Universe. At the level of the Universe *all is one*.

The single most important realization I have had in my life is that the Universe is a whole composed of wholes that are composed of wholes, all rhythmically and systemically balanced so that there is a pervasive unity from the infinitesimal to the infinite.

In 1967, Arthur Koestler coined the word *holon* to describe the part-whole phenomena. A holon is the relationship between entities that are self-complete, wholes and entities that are seen to be dependent parts. To me, they are integral luminescence of beingness. (This is illustrated with graphics in the *To Educate Eco-Sapiens*: see Endnote 128.)

Traveling back through the nested hierarchies within the Universe, there are holons of galaxies. Our Milky Way galaxy embraces star system holons, one of which contains the holon of planet Earth, where a diversity of systems are an interplay, a vibrating dance of holonic entities. Our holonic Universe expresses itself through differentiation, autopoiesis, and communion, creating a chaotic, yet consistently dynamic, balance throughout the cosmos. Our Earth, Gaia, expresses that same systemic-holographic structure.

If you take one idea from this chapter I hope it is this:

You have a visceral connection
From the holon

That is you
Through all the systemic holons
That constitute your body as an integral holon
of Earth, solar system, and cosmos.
Feel it and know its truth.

If you pass that sense of being in the world on to children and adults in your sphere of influence, you will be engaging in a process of furthering the evolution of eco-sapiens.

Except for a six-month interlude when I was 11 years old, my education was not holistic. And I was consistently searching for integration and origins. That is why I chose science as my vocation. Science became my mediator to counsel me. I grew up in urban New York City with little or no kinship to natural environments or cosmos. My childhood was void of visceral experiences of being in nature, so science provided the language to help me see the systemic intercomplexities of Earth and Cosmos.

Most people are so far removed from the natural world that they have lost their visceral connection – their holonic connection – to it. Consequently our organizations and communities are based on mechanistic, hierarchical structures, without flow and integration. While exploring schools, personal relationships, individual lives – and noticing the dance of Gaian functioning – one might observe parts of the tapestry that are present as well as parts that are missing. What is the stability point? What function unifies the relationships? What is the partnership that contributes to the whole? What is the matrix: resources from which everything arises? What built-in system – the feedback function – balances the whole? How do things grow and change? And what provides the energy for the network?

Our human ancestors did not have science to help them understand their relationships. They were embedded in the natural systems and did not need definitions. The question arises: In what ways might modern humans in their personal relationships, communities, and organizations function if we had maintained our dynamic balance with nature?

Building on the ecological functions of natural systems, Marsha and I began exploring how this perspective might be applied to human systems of organization – even individual lives or personal relationships (see Chapter Seven). We spent more than 15 years analyzing communities as well as our personal lives using the perspective of ecological functions. Marsha had direct experience of a holographic Universe. She reasoned that human communities are derivative holons of the whole Earth system of ecological networks – with the same propensities for organization. Even if applied metaphorically, it could lead to deeper awareness. While Marsha was developing her approach to natural mapping, Janine Benyus first introduced the idea of biomimicry.[142]

In 2014, Marsha's illness progressed to a point that I could no longer care for her. This disorientation drove me into my personal creativity river to contextualize our collaborative work. It is from this vantage point that I began to explore the core question that drives this book.

The natural map holon shown in Figure 8 is a result of that exploration. It describes the relationships that compose Gaian education. We did not set out with this intention; it only revealed itself to me as I began to explore each of our histories of working with children and adults. In 1998, a student in our Integrative Learning M.Ed. told us that we had created "Montessori for adults." We looked at each other, recognizing it was not by design, but understandable because Montessori insights formed the core of who we were, and working with adults was not that much different than working with children.

Education
A Systems View for Gaian Renewal

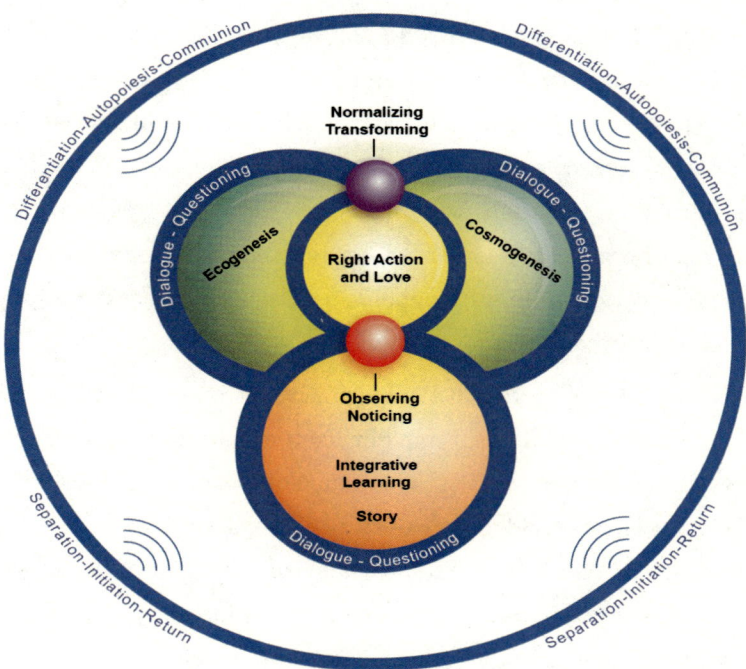

Figure 8. Natural Map of To Educate Eco-Sapiens

I begin with the unity function; occupying that space is right-action and love. In our work with children and adults, we observe three emergent qualities:

- **Cosmophilia** – the overwhelming awe one feels for the Universe, not merely its beauty, but the incredible complex processes that manifest the unimaginable.
- **Ecophilia** – the tendency to bond with the natural world and to notice/feel the presence of Earth systems that sustain life.
- **Biophilia** – the instinctive love for the living world.

Right-action arises from the Buddhist notion of *dharma*. Along with right-live-lihood and right-speech, it forms the ethical contract we have that arises from our truth. Thomas Berry's notion of Great Work and Maria Montessori's idea of Cosmic Task emanate through right-action and love.

The partnership function includes context-setting, ecogenesis, and cosmogenesis. As I alluded to earlier, the starting place for comprehending our place within the holarchies of cosmos and ecos is seeing-feeling our relationship to Gaia. Marsha used ecogenesis to describe a fundamentally new perspective based on a holistic-ecological view rather than on a hierarchical, mechanistic, or patriarchal model. During the last 100 years, we have moved from a sense of cosmos to cosmogenesis, the understanding that there is a continuous unfolding of relationship-communion throughout space and time, that everything that exists is a derivative of this process.

When I left engineering in 1973 to pursue a career in education I believed that if people understood the overarching contexts they would come to know that everything is interconnected in a meticulous web of relationships – and that this knowledge would change the way we behave toward each other and toward the Earth. As I said earlier, I was only partially right. *Knowledge itself is not enough.* There needs to be congruent, seamless processes that allow learners to live in those contexts and develop right-action.

Integrative learning and story hold the space of the matrix function in our natural map for Gaian education. I have already addressed the importance of story for establishing contexts as well as the use of exploratory questioning to assuage conditioning and unexamined assumptions. Some additional aspects of integrative learning include: creative expression, non-adversarial relationships, acknowledging intuition and heart wisdom, formation of a dynamic learning community, and personal-interest driven research.

During my preparation to become a teacher, I experienced a noticable inequality between the methods used in teacher education and the approaches we were told to use with children. As addressed earlier, I was chosen to be one of those who would "train" Montessori teachers and then resigned in a search for the missing congruence. Today, the TIES faculty embraces this congruence in working with adult learners.

I have placed dialogue and questioning as the feedback loop that inter-penetrates the other functions. As shared earlier, dialogue is a process that begins with a willingness to be tentative about what you know, and its focus is on "what is" rather than on ideas and opinions. At the beginning of our graduate program we share the following guidelines:

- Dialogue starts from a willingness to be tentative about what you know.

- The focus of dialogue is on "what is" rather than on ideas and opinions.

- Dialogue is letting the issue unfold with affection and mutual respect.

- When a reaction arises, neither suppress nor defend it, but stay with it and let it unfold, keeping it constantly, observing, and question-ing. Dialogue is "being together" and "seeing together" in an unfold-ing relationship.

- Dialogue is not "agreeing or disagreeing," nor is it convincing or arguing.

- Dialogue is a way to create a new culture of meaning. It involves new habits of being with a group and of being with yourself. The purpose of dialogue is to pursue collective learning and shared meaning.

Exploratory questions encourage dialogue. They are open-ended and replace expository inquiries that require arguments and justification. In exploratory writing, the student takes the reader on a journey, sharing what has been learned through study and experience. Exploratory questions usually begin with "How might...?" or "In what ways...?" or "What possibilities are there for...?" These kinds of questions also propagate deep reflection and expose assumptions that might assist in the unconditioning process.

In Aikido, there is the idea of one-point, which is the emanating place for your statement of intention. It is a place without thought, yet all knowl-edge-wisdom resides there. It is a place of balance and seeing. Gaia's one-point is the soil.

The referenced natural map illustrates the relationships in education for Gaian renewal: To Educate Eco-sapiens. The stability point (Gaia's one-point) for the rising education is observing and noticing. These are quiet, internal

– even spiritual – processes that help center oneself in order to sustain one's vision. They are imbued with the intelligence of love as an omnipresent force, and allow for perceiving the "what is" without influence of past or future and without judgment or interpretation. Emergent "truth" may lead to right-action.

Differentiation, autopoiesis, and communion hold the place of the energy function. These tendencies, born in the birth of cosmic unfolding, continue to precipitate dynamic balance throughout time and space for ongoing manifestation within the holons of creation. I have added to this outside circle separation, initiation, and return as processes that are imbedded in the human psyche for personal as well as species transformation.

The last function – the growth point – in our ecological Gaian metaphor for education is held by normalizing and transforming. For years I had objections to the Montessori use of the word normalization. I thought it old-fashioned, archaic, and not descriptive. Within a very short time period, three experiences changed my perspective.

First, I read copies of letters gifted to me by Binda Goldsbrough. Mario and Maria Montessori sent these letters (see Appendix III) to her in September 1939, just before they left for India (25 October 1939), and only a few months before the Nazi invasion of Holland. Mario tells her "... in times such as these anything may happen. In case the worst arrives and you survive, form a group with a few others – who have Mammolina in their soul." And, "Make sure no one forgets the period of normalization because that will lead the child to become a conscious master of all its faculties." (Mammolina was a term of endearment used by members of the family.) Mario also mentions the Swedenborg movement. Emmanuel Swedenborg was a mystic, an architect, a spiritual teacher from the 18th century, and Mario said that he hoped that Montessori would someday be as popular as that movement. For Swedenborg, love is the essence of spiritual fire.

I think Mario's reminder from just before World War II is just as true today as it was in 1939: "Do not let the present mar your mind and your soul; retain that freshness of spirit and that love that are so necessary to carrying out our work." And he goes on to address how his mother's ideas are transformative and necessary for the future of humanity. "I trust to God that you and others – who are our spiritual children – may find in your love and in your intelligence the means of making Mammolina's message and work penetrate [human]kind's soul."

Then I had an experience with a massage therapist who practiced *tui-na* – in my neck. When I could talk again, I asked him what he was doing. He told me he was normalizing the tissue. I inquired as to what he meant by that term, and he explained that it means returning the tissue to its normal state.

Finally, I came across normalization one more time in dialogue with a colleague. She used the term normalizing in reference to helping clients restore their psychological and emotional health.

If normalizing means creating an atmosphere that enables one to return to a normal state, does that infer that it might lead to an unconditioned state of unfolding consciousness? What might that look like in education? Normalization was used by Maria Montessori to describe a state of focused attention wherein certain human attributes emerge that provide heightened awareness of self and self in relationship with other. Might normalizing be an ongoing process, one that occurs over a lifetime, not just in childhood?

To respond to that question, I explored excerpts from our graduate student's papers and other reflections in seminars. In their writing, I observed the emergence of passion, social awareness, inner freedom, internal coherence, altruistic behavior, and the corollary qualities of empathy and humility. My conclusion is that the normalizing process applies to all ages and is key to transforming self and self-in-relationship to Gaia.

In addition to normalizing qualities, we see transformative process. This is the creative power in an educational experience that empowers individuals to find deeper meaning in their lives in order to contribute to the greater good.

Taking this natural map of Gaian education as a whole, I come away with the understanding that TIES is a Montessori graduate school. It follows the underlying vision for a university as described by Maria Montessori during the late 1930s. It is Montessori for adults in both content and process and is applicable, not just to Montessori teachers, but also across most disciplines.

I believe people have a deep calling beyond individual and family. It is where their gifts and the world's needs intersect. From a spiritual perspective, it is our inner journey.

Whatever the name, it is the invisible evolutionary thread-connection or cord of causation that carries us forward from ancestral generations to the here and now and beyond into our collective futures.

CHAPTER ELEVEN:
EXTENDING THE MONTESSORI VISION

The creators of (the TIES) curriculum beautifully integrated the philosophies and principles of Maria Montessori by holistically weaving them together in order to address and remedy our current planetary crisis. – TIES Student

The TIES program embodies Montessori principles by following the needs of the adult learner, by creating an environment of respect, featuring self-directed learning, exploration and hands-on learning activities. The program challenges adults to start noticing, looking, observing, creating, and learning. –TIES Student

Experimentation and innovation are the essence of the TIES tradition, as they have steadfastly manifested their vision much in the manner that New England poet Mary Oliver describes as "lifting the hoof of an idea." Philip Snow Gang and Marsha Snow Morgan had a vision, seeded by passion, and they, idea by idea, step by step, built it into a viable, innovative, transformative pathway for adult learners. TIES was an online pioneer in education, discovering the power of digital communities through the simplicity and beauty of meaningful dialogic relationships. Each year seemed to bring yet another consideration, an experiment, upgrade or innovation. – Enid Larsen (See Appendix IV)

Before writing this book the question kept rising up, why me? As I began sharing this with people who knew me well, the response was "You are the one. Who else could write it?" Tamara Castleman, my muse and editor for this project wrote:

> It is the story of your own driving question. And then that question unfolds in your life as a Montessori teacher-educator. And you have personal stories as a friend of the Montessori family: Maria Montessori's son, Mario Sr., granddaughter Renilde, grandson Mario, Jr., and great-granddaughter Carolina. Not only this, but you came to the Montessori scene when there were still first-generation Montessori educators who worked directly with her, notably Binda Goldsbrough, an assistant to Maria Montessori before and after World War II. Binda bequeathed to you copies of letters she received from the Montessoris just before they left Europe for India in 1939. They reveal core essences.
>
> And you have always had an interest in roots and contexts, and you have that letter from Mario, Jr.

The letter that Tamara refers to, is the one Mario, Jr. wrote about me in 1980 (Chapter Five) where he says that I am "a dedicated person … enterprising; with a realistic outlook; not giving up easily but recognizing the limitations presented by a given situation and abiding by them until a new opportunity offers itself to bring whatever he is doing a step further." I received similar encouraging letters from Mario, Sr. I now know that both Mario, Sr., and Mario, Jr. recognized things about me four decades ago that I did not see myself; and I understand now why it is important for me to share and extend the Montessori legacy.

In this chapter I will integrate what I have learned over the years as an educator and independent researcher with what I know about Montessori teaching and learning "to bring what I have been doing a step further," as Mario wrote. But first, some background is needed before I address my work with adults over the last 35 years.

From 1907 forward Maria Montessori devoted her life to childhood education, at first concentrating on children under 6 years of age, which she later named the first developmental plane. During the 1930s and 1940s, along with her son Mario, she developed a more comprehensive plan for educating the second plane of development: children between 6 and 12 years of age. She describes the first plane as a period of rapid growth and self-construction, while the second plane is a time for consolidation, making meaning of the world.[143] As I mentioned earlier, her ideas for adolescence were formed during the mid 1930s. Mario Montessori, Jr. told me that Jur Haak,[144] who later became a teacher of mathematics and physics, co-founded the Montessori Lyceum Amsterdam. He also tried to implement Erdkinder in Holland but the war intervened. Montessori identifies the period from 12 to 18 years of age as the third plane of development – the birth of the social being and a time of social construction. As for the fourth plane of development, ages 18 to 24, Montessori called this a period of consolidation with the rise of the mature adult. Sometime in 1939 she wrote the article "The Function of the University" where she explains:

> This world . . . needs a "new human."
>
> Spontaneous collaboration in all manifestations of life is a fact that has come as a true revelation. Association gives new strength by stimulating the energies. To act in association with others either in thought or in practice is the only way in which human nature can be active.[145]

I have copious notes taken from reading that lecture years ago, but at the time it did not cross my mind that I would be extending the Montessori wisdom into work with adults, arriving at an insight into a fifth plane of development. Over the last 35 years while working with adult learners I have had a very strong feeling that something arises between the ages of 24 and 30 that has the potential to initiate people on a lifelong learning journey – one that embraces their Great Work. That certainly was the case with me during the late 1960s with the birth of my children, discovery of Montessori, and the civil unrest that permeated the culture. I have had many informal interviews with friends, students, graduates, and faculty and without exception all of them can name a significant event (or events) that occurred during this fifth plane of development. For some, the event ignited a flame that was already burning in their hearts, while for others it was a rapid awakening or calling to do something dramatically different, something that involved contributing to Earth's well-being. I think this "something" is a touchstone set of experiences that acknowledges the journey of the self toward the Self.

It surprised both Marsha and me when Cynthia Burns, a TIES student in 1998, told us we had created "Montessori for adults." I had been working with adults giving seminars and courses for decades before the graduate program started and carried those contexts and processes into the Masters of Education course of study. Now I can tell the story of that experience.

———————◆———————

During reflection and meditation, I often get a glimpse and witness the meaningful threads that have been woven together during my lifelong journey. Sometimes I smile when I see spirit and causation mingling for active expression. I had no way of knowing what might unfold in 1988 when I made the decision to leave my position as head of school as well as turn away from Montessori organizations, which included dropping out of the preparation to become a Montessori "official" teacher-educator… with all its organizational constraints. Without any plan, the threads began to weave themselves. I was at once invited to give seminars in Auckland, Sydney, and Melbourne, and then Stockholm and Helsinki. These seminars, *Transforming Education: A Planetary Approach*, were organized around holistic education, sustainability, and global awareness. With the emergence of GATE, in 1990 I was invited to speak all over the world. (I literally kept a suitcase ready to go.) These offerings and experiences included sharing the *Education 2000* vision (see Appendix II) during the symposium I developed: *"Leadership for Transforming Education: A Holistic-Ecological Shift."*

The work of GATE was key to the emergence of the TIES graduate programs in Integrative Learning and Montessori Integrative Learning. Wherever I gave GATE presentations it was inevitable that the question would arise "Where can I study more about this vision for education?" As a result of these travels my network of like-minded, kindred spirits throughout the world grew rapidly. It was during these years that Marsha and I looked into each other's eyes and knew there was a calling for co-creation; we just did not know how we would get there. Despite the obstacles, we persevered and engaged in two decades of creative expression – in our relationship and revealing itself through our work in the world. From 1994 - 1997 we created and facilitated the symposium *Paradigma: Learning Communities and the New Science.*

Marsha was a "student" in the first TIES graduate offering, but she was really a co-creator. It was a challenging role but Marsha danced it with perfect poise culminating with the thesis, *"An Ecogenesis for Education: Perceiving Systemic Patterns in the Design and Creation of Learning Communities."*[146] The insights shared in her paper clearly found their way into the process-structure for the TIES graduate program. Looking back on our own years of working with children we both recognized that we had created *learning communities* way before the terminology was coined. The threads that make up TIES' Indra's Net are the processes we embrace to create a community of learners. It is the cosmic energy that is embedded in the journey and reveals itself through dialogue.

I want to visit some of the keynote features of the TIES program and consider how they might align with the Montessori approach.

In the December 2019 issue of *The Sun*, author and essayist, Barry Lopez, describes how a flock of starlings self-organize in flight formation without a leader. He calls it "an aggregate of birds."[147] And then he says,

You must rid yourself of the idea that only one person knows, and understand that genius might be manifest in one man or one woman in a particular moment, but the quality of the genius that characterizes humanity is actually possessed by the community. It might rise up and become real for a single person in the group, but it doesn't belong solely to that person.[148]

Learning Communities

In 1989 I attended a retreat featuring the author of *The Fifth Discipline*, Peter Senge, a system scientist and management lecturer who had written rather extensively about learning organizations. Senge's thesis was that organizations have a flow-through of interdependent relationships that is best modelled systemically where each member of the team contributes to everyone's learning. This was so very familiar to me as I had a history of creating non-hierarchical classroom environments that embrace cooperation, collaboration, and sharing. Those were the guiding process principles included during the many seminars and workshops I gave for adults in the 1980s.

In education circles the term "learning community" was adopted during the early '90s by academic programs based on a cohort structure especially at the graduate level. My initial practice inside a graduate learning community began in 1993 when I was faculty-mentor for doctoral students enrolled in the School for Transformative Learning at California Institute of Integral Studies (CIIS). This was one of the first online doctoral programs. Included in student assessment criteria was a "group demonstration of excellence." My experience with that requirement was significant because I observed how pressure to collaborate can have a negative influence on the process and outcome. However, I learned a great deal during these years about establishing a learning community in an online environment, which, to my surprise, was pregnant with unforeseen coherence.

From 1984 through 1987, my own doctoral studies at The Union Institute and University began as a learning collective, but living far apart and without the Internet, each of us took an individual, self-directed journey through the program. The gift I received in the Union process was the importance of personal ownership of content during tertiary[149] studies. When we established the TIES graduate programs, we combined *both* of my graduate-level experiences in the following ways: (1) We imbedded the core curriculum within the collaborative learning community structure. (2) We gave the students freedom of choice to select their own "emphasis areas" where they explore and research a subject of personal interest. (3) This area is investigated through the lens of what they study in the core program. The whole community thereby learns from each other's inquiries. Here is a reflection that Marsha wrote as a student:

> My experience was and continues to be one of feeling that I was
> part of a mosaic that was created by each person in the community
> contributing through their emphasis perspective to the richness
> of the mix. I did not have to research all of my areas of interest;
> someone else would do it and bring for all to share.[150]

This is reminiscent of my experiences as a Montessori elementary teacher where, although there is common core content, students are always engaged in personal projects, exploring topics their interest and imaginations are drawn toward. At each level of age-specific organization in Montessori schools, children and adolescents model this same integration.

Fostering a graduate cohort as a learning community starts at the very beginning of the program with an introduction to *dialogue* as well as on-campus writing guidelines. These guidelines set the principles for how we commune together. They include practices such as: students' initial written responses integrating reflections on the readings/viewings; subsequent responses that "weave" the thoughts expressed by others in the group; integrating personal experience with theoretical understanding; and posing "questions worth thinking about." These practices are critical to the graduate learning process as they are seamlessly applied to the process of writing exploratory academic papers, raising questions as much as sharing new understanding. A TIES graduate writes: "During the TIES program I was able to take risks and investigate new areas and thought patterns as an explorer because I gained the skills to learn how to learn and how to ask meaningful questions."

Another student reflects on her experience as part of a learning community:

> One of the most innovative aspects of the program is the opportunity it provides for students to become members of a learning community – exchanging ideas, problem-solving, and dialogue with students and faculty from diverse cultures and countries. My community included students from Indonesia, Denmark, New Zealand, Latvia, and the United States.

While there is widespread interchange among cohort members and faculty, the faculty ensure that students are individually recognized for their contributions in the seminar spaces. No one is left out, so there is a sense of belonging. The learning community goes through stages of its own development as students experience the environment as non-adversarial and a safe place to share their truth.

Our experience with using dialogue in the online environment has been quite extraordinary. Since there is a built-in time delay between postings and responses, students and faculty have the time to pause and reflect in order to really listen and understand. Exchanges flow, weaving a tapestry of sorts. Unlike traditional, in-person classrooms, the online campus helps to draw all participants into contributing because one is not "seen" unless one posts a written response. Since there is a limit to the number of postings per student over a seminar period, the learning community is not dominated by a few people.

When dialogue is the form of energy exchange, a sense of community and a non-competitive, supportive environment arises where students feel comfortable sharing their ideas and celebrating classmates' milestones. In one student's evaluation of the program, she shares: "TIES promotes relationships among persons across continents and this brings great richness to how one perceives the world. Never before had I established such deep ties with colleagues or as deep learning as I experienced in this program."

Cosmic Education

In my experience, learning communities evolve and consciousness is touched when the inquiry is imbedded in meaningful contextual relationships. Knowing our cosmic evolutionary journey and exploring how humanity is part of the web of life seems primary to an understanding of who you are and why you are here. It provides a sense of belonging to the Universe with the keynote of responsibility for "giving back" to the web of life. Visiting faculty, Lauren deBoer explains (see Appendix VI), "This allows one to navigate the tensions between the smaller self one inherits from family and culture and the greater Self that calls us to transcend ideology and belief and embrace the larger whole of the cosmic community." Montessori spent the last two decades of her life exploring the realm of cosmic ideas. At first it was just for the teachers to understand that everything on Earth forms a systemic whole and that every creature has an unconscious contribution to make by *giving back* to the whole. That is, except for modern humans who need learning experiences to viscerally understand the systemic nature of life on Earth. Later, with her son at her side, they developed an approach to presenting this synthesis to elementary-aged children.

Cosmic Education – is shared through story during the younger years and through science later on. It is an orientation to the cosmos and the cosmogenetic principles of differentiation, autopoiesis, and communion. *Cosmos* and *Gaia* are the overarching contexts for imbeddedness in the TIES graduate program. In this way students come to understand the human journey, and, at the same time they contemplate their own role as an educator. A graduate shares, "Because of my experience in the TIES program I'm more consciously aware of expressing and living a life of thankfulness and gratitude for our heritage in order to help create a sustainable future."

The sense of discovering their own passion is personally experienced at the end of the second semester when students study Joseph Campbell's *Hero's Journey*, followed by exploring Thomas Berry's *Great Work*. I have been surprised how often students and graduates –experiencing the cycles of separation, initiation, and return – have also written about TIES as a hero's journey.

Cosmic Education is the context for Integrative Learning because it is the foundation for personal right-action born out of understanding.

Integrative Learning

I vividly remember returning from Europe in 1974 with a suitcase of three-ring binders filled to capacity with lessons for children, as well as the philosophy behind the Montessori approach. There were eight separate albums: Mathematics One and Two, Language, Geography, Geometry, History, Biology, and Psychology-Philosophy. They contained more than 1000 presentations and lessons. We were told "It's all connected," but were never given any clues as to how to integrate the different areas of inquiry in the classroom. That took many years of working with children. It made me acutely aware that unless teachers experience interconnectivity in their teacher preparation, it is challenging to pass it on to the students they teach.

When Marsha and I were designing how the first cohort would encounter the work, we did not say, "Let's design a learning community," or "Let's use integrative learning as a unifying function." We developed the content and designed the process; then looked at what we created before naming it *integrative learning*. At the time, the term was not being used as a marker in education: We wanted a name with a new identity. Marsha and I had been Montessori teachers for many years and that experience translated seamlessly into creating learning environments for adults where integrative learning is primary. Six years before the TIES initiative, Marsha and I organized two innovative Montessori courses in Oslo and Vancouver where we created a community of learners in which group inquiry and questioning were valued. Students formed triads where each member of the triad participated in demonstrations with three different instructors, charging them afterwards with teaching the others in their triad and developing links between lessons. Philosophy and theory were given in a whole group format followed by dialogue.

Integrative learning is introduced as process right from the beginning of the TIES program. Over the initial six months, students apply their learning during context-setting seminars. The readings and viewings explore the following contexts:

- dialogue as a worldview for communicating
- the story of the Universe and its implications for humanity
- holistic education
- self and other observation – exploring assumptions that arise
- understanding the systemic nature of life on Earth and implications for Gaia theory

As students respond to these topics, they integrate the content of videos and/ or books that they have read for each seminar, and, then, when they read other student's postings, they have the opportunity to integrate what others learned in their experiences. They also have private annotation spaces to post quotations that they find important and might later use in academic papers. This initial semester is the first of three phases of inquiry.

During the next six months of study, students explore the thought structures of an integrative world view. The academic focus is on education, philosophy, personal psychology, and the future of humanity. And they are introduced to creativity as a portal between observation and research. The learning community itself is going through a metamorphosis and operates with increasing autonomy, trusting its own voice. This is the second phase of inquiry.

The last six months of study is a time for looking at the tapestry of learning that has been experienced and taking personal ownership to contribute. This contribution is a Culminating Project that reflects the student's passionate interest or Great Work. During this third phase of inquiry the students demonstrate what they have learned and create original projects from their new understanding.

As described earlier, Montessori adapted the notion of the three-period lesson from the work of Édouard Séguin. A few years ago, while assembling the response for the TIES 10-year academic review, I noticed that without orchestrating the three-period lesson as a goal in our work with adults, we had embraced it unconsciously. Perhaps Séguin, in his work with intellectually challenged children more than 150 years ago, tapped into this way of "holistic" learning that lies underneath the surface of all integrative knowing. In Montessori circles the three periods are:

(This is...) the teacher names the quality or object and makes the necessary associations.

(Show me...) the teacher still furnishes the name, but the child must recognize it.

(What is this?) children now verbalize what they have learned.

The three semester phases in the TIES graduate program are directly related to Séguin and Montessori's three period lesson.

This is integrative learning emanating from the question, "What is the context for integrative earning?

Show me integrative learning derives from the question, "What is the philosophy of integrative learning?"

What is integrative learning responds to, "In what ways can we apply integrative learning in our own lives as well as the community we work with?"

The Idea of Freedom within Limits

Students create self-organized supplemental material that informs their individual area of emphasis. They ask many questions – especially in the first phase – and are provided ample opportunity to make self-discovery possible. Although there is no traditional grading structure, the program is designed with many firm boundaries.

Observation, Creativity, and Research

Central to integrative learning is observation, creativity, and research as reflective inquiry. Students explore the nature of observation and engage in creative processes to further self-observation and intuitive insight. This enables students to create similar experiences for the children or adults they work with. Montessori's approach to learning with children was born out of her own unprejudiced observation. She recognized that observation is a fundamental way of knowing. TIES has extended that knowing by applying a research methodology that uses third- and first- person analyses to explore relationship in an educational setting. One not only observes other, but also observes self, and self observing other, which in many instances leads to integration and transformation. Our research is focused on what happens in a healthy educational setting where the participants establish a relationship with the learning environment, which includes other children, the teachers and the learning materials. It is the essence of autopoiesis. A graduate explains:

> TIES helped me to see the interplay between subjective and objective realities as the realm in which to search for truth and meaning. It was the first time in my life that I had an opportunity to explore a level of structure to my thoughts on the nature of consciousness.

Indirect and Direct Preparation

Norman was 11 years old and had been in Montessori school since he was three. Using the trinomial cube,[151] I introduced him to the process of calculating cube root. One day, after he had practiced for over a week, he came to me with a revelatory expression and said, "Now I know what a cube is!" Norman's initial introduction to cube-ness came when he was three years old and was given a lesson with the pink tower.[152] The direct aim or purpose of this exercise is to help with visual and tactile discernment of different dimensions. Among many of the indirect aims is the nurturing and development of a mathematical mind. Norman frequently encountered cubes over the next eight years, but it was as if he "discovered" their essence when he learned how derive the cube root and discerned that the root is the length of a side.

Many students in our graduate program identify points of consciousness and insight during the last semester when they are able to reflect upon all the previous experiences that led to their new understanding. I attribute much of this to the natural sequences and flows that build conceptual foundations and awareness for comprehending more complex ideas and relationships later in the program. This process is not linear but spiral-like where new concepts are seen as integrated passages.

A prime example of this is the four-week observation experience during the first semester. A direct aim of this activity is to observe without prejudice, identifying personal assumptions that impact what is seen. Another aim is to experience how to observe self while observing other. Creativity seminars later in the program emphasize the same third- and first- person observations, and then in the last semester the students study a neurophenomenological approach to research, which is an adaptation of third- and first-person awareness. This research process is quite approachable as the core ideas have been slowly revealed throughout their studies. Hence, the first semester observations are an indirect preparation for research. A student explains, "Discussions easily relate to previously read material because of the strategic manner in which each reading has been sequenced. It is truly a systemically prepared online environment."

Dialogue

Metaphorically, dialogue is truly a river running through the lives of student and faculty. The direct aim of introducing this form of communication during the first few weeks of the program is to help catalyze a non-hierarchical, non-adversarial community of learners. Once the community has felt-experiences[153] in this process, it permeates the campus. After his first year of monitoring the program and facilitating two seminars, holistic educator Paul Freedman observed (see Appendix V), "The TIES syllabi have the courage and wisdom to seek out what is most important, the very essence of what it means to be human and live well upon this Earth."

Dialogue also influences the way students respond in their integrative papers at the end of each semester. These papers are written with a tentative, exploratory voice. Driven by reflective questions, they are investigative in the absence of trying to prove something.

Role of the Educator (Teacher, Guide, Facilitator, Mentor)

I think when Maria Montessori writes, ". . . the first step to take in order to become a Montessori teacher is to shed omnipotence, and become a joyous observer,"[154] she is at once decentralizing the learning environment so that it is not dependent on the dominance and knowledge of the teacher. The teacher is a facilitator of learning, understanding the material and concepts, and inviting students into relationship with the learning. The same could be said for working with people of all ages be they children, adolescents, or adults. And what about the notion of the "joyous observer?" I think this joy comes from being able to see without prejudice, as Krishnamurti would say, the unconditioned mind. Because in that state of clarity one can observe and really respond to the situation as it presents itself without any assumptions. This frees the teacher to respond to what-is rather than some formulated pattern to achieve ends.

Early on, Maria Montessori wrote, "It is unquestionable that with this method of education the preparation of the teacher must be made *ex novo* [Latin, meaning "from the beginning"] and that the personality and social importance of the instructress will be transformed thereby."[155] Binda Goldsbrough explained to me in very clear terms that although Maria Montessori could articulate the role of the Directress (teacher) with the children, she did not use that approach when she worked with adults. She trained the teachers using the same methods that she had experienced in her own tertiary education: demonstration and lecture. If the transformation of the teacher is to be made ex novo, then the educator of teachers has to "shed omnipotence" for the self-transformation of the teacher. In the TIES program we are all co-learners on a journey of discovery. Some of us have more experience and knowledge, but everyone can contribute to the whole.

One of the major roles of the teacher is to *prepare the environment*, and not merely in a physical sense. The physical is what usually comes to mind. How do I create spaces that work at this developmental stage? – placement of desks, floor space, shelves, materials – all the physical needs of the classroom. Extrinsic and intrinsic coherence is equally as important as it helps create the psychological and energetic atmosphere you feel when you enter a classroom that is working harmoniously and, one in which even if there are perturbations, things settle and stabilize. How does this happen? And can it evolve in an online environment?

When teaching children, I created community circles as opportunities to share and address interpersonal relationships and resolve issues as they arise. These experiences set a norm for how to commune together. Working with adults in our online environment, the physical design of the campus makes it quite simple to navigate and not get lost in the separate threads that exist with many academic software applications. In fact, our original 1996 campus was designed by social engineers interested in creating online communities.

So how do we create a healthy psychological and energetic atmosphere online? It begins with the discovery of dialogue and how the faculty models the principles in such a way that by the middle of the second semester the students as a whole begin to emerge as leaders of the cohort. The faculty is present to support the students' learning, not to criticize or to judge. If we sense a misunderstanding in an approach to the content, we pose reflective questions like "Have you thought about. . . ?" or "You might consider. . ." In this way students find the answers themselves. It is much like the three-year old who says, "Help me to do it myself."[156] The interactions between all members of the learning community are non-adversarial. In this way students have freedom of expression without judgment, which often stimulates them to explore their own inner realms and assumptions. Years after graduating one of our students wrote:

> TIES made a huge difference in my life: 18 months of not being told I was wrong. That was the first time ever in an academic setting. If I had an idea that was not precisely on course the faculty were so gentle with their suggestions. It enabled me to come to new conclusions on my own. I was not aware of this "steering" or "guiding" process towards right-action until a few years after graduating.

It also helps to have a highly qualified faculty with decades of experience at all levels of working with children and adolescents. They apply academic standards and language to who we are and what we do. The entire faculty's experience and common understanding is a catalyst for seamlessness in our work as a team and in our commitment to ideas we have lived with children, adolescents and adults. Freedman (see Appendix V) explains:

> The faculty open each seminar with such personal and poetic expressions of who they are as human beings, rooted in place and context. They proceed to engage alongside the learners with obvious care, posing key questions in response to students' comments, driving the dialogue ever deeper, in an intricate process known at TIES as "weaving." Often faculty mentors will share new relevant content beyond the syllabus, or add their own reflections, insights and applications of quotes that have been identified by the students. Mentors are willing to expose their own vulnerabilities and not-knowing, always as an invitation to dive deeper together, with awe and wonder. Perhaps most remarkable of all is the mentors' capacity to allow for space and emergence within the dialogue, while still reassuring the community of their watchful caring presence.

The faculty practices third- and first- person observation during their online interactions with students. Just like in a Montessori class for younger people, this observation informs the trajectory of the dialogue by noticing what is needed in a given situation. We enter the dialogue with minimal expectations as to its direction and then observe the *what-is,* allowing for learning to arise in its own evolution. This practice also resonates with my experience as a Montessori teacher of children. Faculty, just like Montessori teachers, know how to ask the right questions to enable students to discover their own answers.

Working with adults in many ways is similar to working with children, but there are major differences. The TIES faculty is attuned to the nuances of the adult learner and often reach out, first by email and then perhaps by phone or teleconference for clarification and personal support. Our students are all working adults and as such have multiple responsibilities, not only in their professional career but also as parents, spouses, and children of older parents. Life happens in the journey of adulthood and the faculty have to be sensitive to these vicissitudes.

I began this chapter with an exploration into the nature of learning communities as primary to integrated learning where content and process are congruent. I shared that the context for integrative learning is Cosmic Education– the sense of the whole and how the individual might contribute to that wholeness. I addressed integrated learning as the framework of the TIES program and then explored:

- *Dialogue* as the flow of meaning among participants.
- *Three phases of learning* that bring to mind the hero's journey.
- *Freedom within limits* to assist in self-construction.
- *Observation, creativity, and research* as an evolving practice to explore individual and collective roles.
- *Indirect preparations* to sow seeds for later integration
- *Role of the educator* to prepare the physical and psychological space for learning and to continuously observe in order to understand.

I think it's important to note that many students continue learning TIES concepts after graduation. One graduate explains:

> I understood the concept of neurophenomenology when I grad- uated. I understood neurophenomenology with added awareness three years later. I think it's apropos to recognize that students don't just find new ways to apply TIES principles, many of them actually keep learning what TIES was teaching. The same applies to children. My daughter has a learning disability in math but found geometry surprisingly easy. When I asked her why she thought that was, she said it was because of the geometric solids in preschool. She said that proofs were easy because she had "taken

all those shapes into my body." She could prove a square based pyramid was square because she felt it. To me that is continuing to learn from Montessori materials.

As I mentioned much earlier in this book, I did not have words to describe the feelings I had when I encountered the Montessori classroom as a parent of a 3 and 7 year old. I just knew that something special was happening, experiencing that "something" as coherent flow. Later on, in my work as a teacher and head of school, I would experience that same classroom flow. It is a visceral sense of being in a safe environment where individual and group activity flowers, both in the domains of interpersonal communication and academic exploration.

And for the last 25 years I have had that same experience as a participant and co-learner in the learning communities that TIES has evolved. Just as I would go into a Montessori classroom when I was head of school – to observe and remember why we do what we do – I often go on to our campus to observe student interactions. I often come away with a sense of *all good things in all good time.* This is a sense of knowing that in good time – at the right moment – things will reveal themselves in a profound way and that patience and observation-awareness are keynotes to this process.

Contextualized Graduate Study

Current science and systems thinking promotes a fundamental change in approach to studying phenomena. The new sciences shift thinking from simply studying experienced phenomena as an objective observer to actively experiencing the phenomena as part of the subject. This shift from the "cause and effect" paradigm, which has been central to the scientific method for centuries was transformed during the 20th century to include the subjectivity of the observer as key to the understanding of the phenomena. To encapsulate this principle, the TIES M.Ed. programs in Integrative and Montessori Integrative Learning contextualize –within contemporary scientific thought and the development of systems thinking– the emergence of an integrative world view. This new meta or cosmic thinking was articulated by Maria Montessori during those 1935-1936 lectures, followed by her years in India (1939-1946).

Two pillars of academic inquiry emerge for the TIES learner-student. deBoer, shares this insight (see Appendix VI),

> TIES is an energizing program in that it provides a sense of place (ecology) and story (cosmology) as the underpinnings of true learning. One's identity is validated because you see yourself situated within the entire order of living things, not outside. One's sense of purpose is validated because you see yourself situated within a story that is still spinning its narrative from the dynamics of evolution and upon which you can have a direct impact because you are as much the story as every other subject. Out of this comes a felt connection to the energy and will of the planet itself and of the unfolding evolutionary process.
>
> It's not only the pillars of ecology and cosmology, but the ambit within which they are explored – respectful listening and dialogue and openness to learning as an individual process super-charged by a community of learners. The invocation of the powers of ecology and cosmology provides an energizing matrix within which the human spirit can be adequately prepared for the challenges and difficulties ahead.

The first pillar is an understanding of the evolution of the Universe. The science of the Universe story has emerged over the last 50 years. Discoveries stemming from cosmogenesis reveal common beginnings from a single unity. Congruent with this idea is that each emergence, including homo sapiens, illustrates that interconnectivity, each event revealing aspects of the originating whole. This awareness of this pervasive unity is a key concept of the TIES program. In the last chapter of her thesis, a student writes:

> Without question, this has been the most enriching formal education experience of my life. The program is a journey of both spiritual and personal growth. The progressive ideas and concepts

garnered from the curriculum emphasize the importance of eco-literacy, interconnectedness, and our relationship to the cosmos.

The second pillar emerges through an understanding of meta and micro-systems on Earth. Before the Gaia Theory was a hypothesis, Maria and Mario Montessori had designed an educational approach based on the premise that the Earth is a whole living system. Gaia theory situates Earth as a meta-system, or an ecology of many systems interacting. Understanding Gaian systems and cosmic origins provide the academic foundation that I named ecocosmology.

Mario Montessori, based on the work he did with his mother while they were in India, developed a Montessori approach to the study of ecology:

> All things which form the environment are connected. After all
> studies are done it can be affirmed that all the Earth and Cosmos,
> from the micro to the macro-organism, are completely joined
> and bound. . . . The child should become so interested that he
> can discover ecosystems for himself. He must realize that there
> are ecosystems within ecosystems . . . There must be harmony
> between all of them for balance to be achieved.[157]

The TIES program is grounded in Montessori's philosophical framework and process. We acknowledge that individuals learn best when provided with the following conditions:

- Opportunities to develop personal responsibility
- Experience empathy and mindfulness
- Work collaboratively with others
- Explore their own creativity
- Receive support and mentoring from specially trained faculty-facilitators

Accordingly, the faculty prepares the online campus with a structure and culture that provides students with individualized learning experiences. Each student, under the guidance of a mentor and other members of the faculty, works independently and takes personal responsibility for learning. In her program summary, one student wrote:

> The ability to manage time well, meet strict deadlines, and contribute professional-level annotations and published-level writing outputs are all a part of the program's underlying requirements. The faculty's natural capacity to coach and see the potential in each student supported my needs to complete the requirements for graduation.

Students access required resources and then meet to share reflections during campus seminars. These readings, viewings, and experiences provide a contextualized content. Mindful learning occurs through this integrative process. Most students experience the program as an integrated whole, rather than a series of disconnected papers, or isolated ideas. Through their sharing, they become aware of others' viewpoints, and are more clearly able to articulate their own perspective. One student writes:

> I felt inspired to be connected to the TIES' faculty, students, and materials because we are all interconnected in a quest to see a more vibrant – viable – and caring Earth community. This program has helped me hone my critical thinking and questioning skills, in addition to delving deeper into any particular subject; approaching a topic from a multidisciplinary perspective.

Visiting the roots of the Montessori approach enables one to create a coherent context. Through scientific observation of young people interacting within an environment provisioned to meet their physical and psychological needs, a strategic organizing principle emerged: knowledge can be attained through contextually developed content, catalyzed by a process-oriented approach that honors the learner's initiative to take responsibility for his/her own learning journey.

That foundation is set into motion through processes that emphasize: seamless integration of all coursework; dialogue as communication and its counterpart exploratory writing; neurophenomenology (observation of self and other); development of a learning community; creativity as expression; skilled questioning wherein learners discover answers on their own; and faculty as mentors acknowledging heart-wisdom. These processes allow the learner to explore and identify with the content of the curriculum through inner and group reflection. Soon after graduating, a student wrote:

> What truly amazed me is how the program was structured in a way
> that supported me emotionally, as if the program developers knew
> exactly what adult learners would experience. With the patient
> guidance and caring support from my mentor I was able to keep
> up with the assignments and projects despite all the challenges
> faced during those 18 months.

A few years before I went to Bergamo, Italy to become a Montessori teacher, my father, interested in his grandchildren's education, asked "But what happens after age 12?" That question placed me on this 50-year-long journey of experimentation and discovery. This is what led me to spearhead the 12-18 exploration in the 1970s and 1980s. I actually started an adolescent program in the mid-1980s but by 1987, as I said earlier, I was exhausted by the politics of Montessori organizations and had to move on. In 1996, when I designed and implemented our graduate programs in integrative learning, I had no idea that Montessori would be imbedded in its process and content, which would evolve into the soul of educating.

CHAPTER TWELVE:
THE SOUL OF EDUCATING

To know your soul's work,
you have to go deep within.

Hope and courage must accompany you on your journey.

To embrace your Great Work,
you have to always create.

This creation of yours is something which
you ultimately become.

Finally you come to realize that
your creation is nothing other than
your self-revelation.[158]

Sri Chinmoy

I am reminded of the Buddhist tradition's eight-fold path of wisdom "that consists of: *right view, right thought, right speech, right action, right mode of living, right endeavor, right mindfulness and right concentration.* 'Right' in this sense means in alignment with divine will, the higher truth."[159] These concepts were articulated over 2500 years ago by the Buddha as a pathway toward self-realization. Might they be similarly a key to the soul of educating? This eight-fold wisdom, when situated in education, focuses on inner development and right-behavior. When Montessori explored the cosmic work of humans, she advocated for humanity to align itself with the rest of life by contributing to nature's balance, rather than diminishing it. Early humans and many indigenous groups practiced this "giving back" unconsciously, but as technological civilization expanded, humanity lost its way in furthering nature's balance. When humans follow their cosmic calling or Great Work they are acting out of *right-behavior*.

The soul of educating restores that right-behavior. Montessori embraces this restorative process in Cosmic Education, which at its root is (1) an understanding of humanity's place in the Universe and (2) right-behavior as a participant in the Gaian community of beings. . . *As Above, So Below.*

The Buddhist eight-fold wisdom of right-behavior is a lens into the root of educating for right-action and love: to understand *humanity's place in the universe* and to *practice right-action as a participant in the Gaian community of beings.* Yes, there are Montessori roots here, too. This is the essence of Montessori's Cosmic Education and cosmic consciousness that I shared in Chapter Nine.

In Aldous Huxley's 1962 utopian novel, *Island,* a school principal explains to a visitor:

> "And let me add, we teach the science of relationship in conjunction with the ethics of relationship. Balance, give and take, no excesses – it's the rule of nature and, translated out of fact into morality, it ought to be the rule among people."[160]

This is the cornerstone of right-action in education and it unfolds in settings that nurture the spiritual essence of the learner.

Earlier, I addressed the normalizing process in the Montessori approach. The qualities of normalization included deep concentration, collaboration, biophilia, love of work, empathy, humility, compassion, independence, cooperation, and love of silence. My observations over the last 50 years have revealed a transformation in the personality of children and adults that have experienced these normalizing qualities. It wasn't until recently that I was able to name some of the emergent attributes of the transformations I have witnessed. They include: Love (as biophilia, ecophilia, and cosmophilia), Hope, Courage, Confidence, Creative Expression, and Gratitude.

Love as biophilia is a sensitivity and respect for life in all its manifestations. Ecophilia, Love of Earth, is evident in the commitment to balance – a sustainable planet. Cosmophilia emerges in our hearts as we comprehend the evolution of the Universe with the awareness that the entire cosmos is interconnected and interdependent – a derivative of one emergent event that makes us descendants of the stars.

Hope lives in cosmophilia with an awareness that balance is the *rule of nature.* Hope arises in non-adversarial learning atmospheres that embrace trust.

Courage, like hope, is also an outgrowth of learning in a trusting environment. It comes to the fore as children and adults have opportunities for individual choice and intuitive decision-making.

Confidence arises when the learning is contextual and sequenced in such a way that learners come to know that they know without someone telling them.

Creative expression emerges when the imagination is fired with inspiration based on experience or intuition. It is an outgrowth of the integration of observation and abstraction.

Gratitude is the all-embracing attribute that arises when one is imbued with Love, Hope, Confidence, and Creative Expression.

I suggest that these five attributes are concrete manifestations that emerge in a prepared environment where the keynote context is Cosmic Education. Indeed they may be vibrations of the soul for the birth of Eco-Sapiens.

Montessori tells us ". . . the child is endowed with unknown powers that can guide us to a radiant future." She continues, "If . . . we really want . . . a new world, then education must take as its aim the development of these hidden possibilities."[161] These hidden possibilities reveal themselves in the prepared environment. If the attributes I have been addressing are cultivated, teacher-guides will be nurturing the embryo for the *new human* that Montessori identified during the last 20 years of her life.

Might the soul of educating be pressing to educate eco-sapiens?

> *We come from cosmos*
> *and we go to cosmos.*
> *Is eternity right here and now?*
> *And is our soul*
> *the one eternal soul*
> *webbed in numinous space and time?*
>
> *As Above, So Below.*

CHAPTER THIRTEEN:
COSMIC GRATITUDE

Breathe in Cosmic love. . .
Breathe out gratitude.

Do not teach: Radiate
Baba Ram Dass [162]

Oh, Divine Spirit of Cosmos and Gaia
And navigator of the river of my life
May I fulfill Your will through
unconditional Surrender,
unconditional Love,

unconditional Compassion,
and unconditional Gratitude.

It is a cold wintery day as I tramp into the nearby forest. A misty rain sweeps through the trees awakening fir, cedar, ivy, moss, fern, and lichen. Gaia proliferates in radiant shades of green. Crow and raven are ever-present and squirrel scurries to and fro. I walk along the footpath that leads me in the direction of Grandmother Cedar. The mist kisses my face and I feel very much alive and welcome. Gratitude pervades my awareness. I reflect on how privileged I have been to have so many firsthand experiences both in the forest and at the sea.

The effervescence of living systems has had a knowing influence throughout my lifelong journey. Gaia has been good to me.

Like the stars above, I am grateful to all the individuals and events that "seemed" to appear in my life at precisely the right time to help me set my sails and navigate the night sky. They influenced the driving question that arose for me, the one that I have responded to throughout this book: *What contexts and processes in education might liberate teachers and learners so that they become catalysts for the new human – one whose integral relationship with Gaia is bound by right-action and love?*

I keep wondering about the source of gratitude. Like consciousness itself, gratitude could not have dropped in with humans. It is a derivative of cosmic evolution. I play with the notion that Gaia herself is grateful for the energy it receives from the Sun to sustain itself. And this energy is pure radiance.

In the beginning the first particles coalesced into hydrogen. As the intensity of this swirling mass increased in its vastness, hydrogen began to fuse into helium releasing the Universe's initial radiance— the light and heat that would make the heavens glow and allow for the birth of all the elements that filled universe. Cosmologist Brian Swimme says, "Every being you encounter contains 13.8 billion years of radiance compressed into it."[163] I see and feel it when I am with forest beings – especially at this time of year in the Pacific Northwest rainforest when the trees and plants are radiant green. I see and feel it when I am at the seaside observing sunrise and sunset or the full moon reflecting over the surface of the waters. Radiance permeates the Gaian land-scape and sometimes can be experienced between humans as we enter into perceiving each other from eye to eye and hand to hand.

So, is there a relationship between gratitude and radiance?

When people like the Dalai Lama or Mother Teresa become attuned to and at peace with the Universal in all its faces, they transcend the typical human experience of living. Being in tune with this Source gives them a luminescence that makes them appear lighter and allows you to see a physical light emanating from them that is indescribable. It feels very good to be in their presence. Thich Nhat Hanh, Buddha, Jesus, they were all expressions of radiance. In listening to Baba Ram Dass, and being with him in person, I could see and feel the radiance. Tradition doesn't matter, connection does. In my own life, Maria Montessori's son and grandson had it, so did Father Divine, as did Robert Muller. With my cosmic love, Marsha, I felt it eyes to eyes, heart to heart, and soul to soul.

Swimme asks:

What do we see when we look into another's eyes? Not at the surface level as empirical details. What is flowing (radiating) out of the eyes is the essence of the person, the fullness of the person. The light itself is the flow of emotion.[164]

And in that flow of emotion I see gratitude. What I have noticed in my own life is when I am with such radiant people I feel in my heart the gratitude that emanates from their eyes.

For me, gratitude is a spiritual expression of profound recognition that is much deeper than appreciation and thankfulness. In Louie Schwartzberg's TED Talk, "Nature, Beauty and Gratitude"[165], he poses that "when we are gobsmacked by a natural scene or event" we often respond by saying:

"Oh, my God." The "Oh" means it caught your attention; the "my" means it connects with something deep within your soul; and "God" is the personal journey we all want to be on, to be inspired, to feel like we are connected to the Universe that celebrates life.

Schwartzberg goes on to explain that "80% of the information we receive comes through our eyes. . . . there is a story behind each face; it's the story of their ancestors." Perhaps there is an essence of cosmic grace that appears through radiance. From my perspective *ancestors* are not limited to the human family, but stretch back through evolutionary time – to the trilobites that invented eyes some 500 million years ago and even further back into deep time from whence we come. That essence is where gratefulness overflows into blessing.

Cosmic gratitude recognizes the spiritual significance of events and people that have contributed to the journey of the self towards the Self. It is born in the radiance that permeates the Universe as it is a reflection of the grace that endows evolution. From our origins in the flaring forth through intergalactic phenomena and Earthly events, I see an unfolding of holarchies of gratitude. For most of my life I have been exploring the multitude of events and experiences that have given us the privilege to appreciate the beauty of the Earth. I recall these words spoken by Brian Swimme during Marsha's and my 2003 dialogue with him: "As an image for exploring Montessori education and the story of the Universe, you might think of part of your journey as releasing your bodies into responding directly to the intelligence that pervades the Earth, Gaia, and the Universe."[166]

We humans have the potential for cosmic gratefulness – that level of gratitude that comprehends the miracle of evolutionary unfoldment. Here and now I think about some of the events that contributed to the articulation of my driving question:

For the Divine timing of the Universe's expansion 13.8 billion years ago, that would have resulted in a total collapse had the speed been a millisecond slower; or total randomness without differentiation if a millisecond faster, I offer gratitude.

For the fusion of three atoms of helium in the belly of star formation 12.9 billion years ago that gave rise to carbon without which there would be no life, I offer gratitude.

For the formation of our supernova 4.6 billion years ago that became our ancestral home; and for that supernova's capacity to create all the elements needed for life on the third planet that revolves around the Sun in our solar system, I offer gratitude.

For the formation of Saturn, whose gravity field tugged on Jupiter just enough, preventing it from moving closer to the Sun and devouring the inner planets including Earth, I give gratitude.

For the Mars-sized planetesimal that collided with the Earth 4.5 billion years ago and created the moon, I offer gratitude. Without the moon Earth would have evolved with a wobbly vertical axis and life as we know it would not have been possible.

For the cyanobacteria, Earth's first photosynthetic beings 3 billion years ago and the eventual formation of a biosphere that created a unitary living planet – Gaia, I offer gratitude.

For our ancestors, the great hominids of the past that learned to survive as Earth's climate shifted and their forest homes disappeared, I offer gratitude for their evolutionary journey that gave birth to culture: language, mathematics, music, and art.

For all of those people in my life – those radiant beings who touched my soul and opened doorways to educating for right-action and love, I offer gratitude.

APPENDIX

I

THE CHICAGO STATEMENT ON EDUCATION

As we approach the twenty-first century, many of our institutions and professions are entering a period of profound change. We in education are beginning to recognize that the structure, purposes, and methods of our profession were designed for an historical period which is now coming to a close. The time has come to transform education so as to address the human and environmental challenges that confront us.

We believe that education for this new era must be holistic. The holistic perspective is the recognition that all life on this planet is interconnected in countless profound and subtle ways. The view of Earth suspended alone in the black void of space underscores the importance of a global perspective in dealing with social and educational realities. Education must nurture respect for the global community of humankind.

Holism emphasizes the challenge of creating a sustainable, just, and peaceful society in harmony with the Earth and its life. It involves an ecological sensitivity - a deep respect for both indigenous and modern cultures as well as the diversity of life forms on the planet. Holism seeks to expand the way we look at ourselves and our relationship to the world by celebrating our innate human potentials - the intuitive, emotional, physical, imaginative, and creative, as well as the rational, logical, and verbal.

Holistic education recognizes that human beings seek meaning, not just fact or skills, as an intrinsic aspect of their full and healthy development. We believe that only healthy, fulfilled human beings create a healthy society. Holistic education nurtures the highest aspirations of the human spirit.

Holistic education is not one particular curriculum or methodology; it is a set of working assumptions that include the following:

- Education is a dynamic and open human relationship.
- Education cultivates a critical awareness of the many contexts of learners' lives - moral, cultural, ecological, economic, technological, political.
- All persons hold vast multi-faceted potentials, which we are only beginning to understand. Human intelligence is expressed through diverse styles and capacities, all of which we need to respect.
- Holistic thinking involves contextual, intuitive, creative, and physical ways of knowing.
- Learning is a lifelong process. All life situations may facilitate learning.
- Learning is both an inner process of self-discovery and a cooperative activity.
- Learning is active, self-motivated, supportive, and encouraging of the human spirit.
- A holistic curriculum is interdisciplinary, integrating both community and global perspectives.

Adopted by 80 Holistic Educators at a
Conference near Chicago, Illinois, June, 1990
Steering Committee: Ed Clark, Phil Gang, David Lehrman,
Linda McRae Campbell,
Nina Meyerhof, Ron Miller, Joey Tanner, Lynn Stoddard.

II

EDUCATION 2000: A Holistic Perspective [167]

1. The fundamental purpose of *education is human growth and development.* Learning involves the enrichment and deepening of relationships to one's inner self, to family and community members, to the global community and to the Earth.

2. Each individual is inherently creative, has unique physical, emotional, intellectual and spiritual needs and abilities, and possesses an unlimited capacity to learn. Education that recognizes learners as unique and valuable, *honors students as individuals.*

3. Learning is an active multisensory engagement between person and world. The *central role of experience* is to engage and immerse learners in the natural and social world as well as their inner world. Curriculum and learning materials support but do not substitute for these vital human relationships.

4. *Systemic thinking* celebrates the full range of human potentials and multiple ways of knowing. It is whole thinking which carries significant implications for human and planetary ecology and evolution. Sustainability has emerged as the keynote for survival in the coming century.

5. The *new role of educators* includes the facilitation of learning, which is an organic, natural process. When educators are open to their own inner being, they invite a co-learning, co-creating process with the learner. In this process, the teacher is learner, the learner is teacher.

6. Genuine education can only take place in an atmosphere of trust. In *reciprocal trust* there is an atmosphere of innovation, care and commitment. This includes freedom of expression and inquiry. Schools should nurture the development of compassionate learning communities.

7. To *educate for a participatory democracy* means that the learning environment must itself revolve around empathy, shared human needs,

justice, and the encouragement of original, critical thinking. Indeed, this is the essence of true education.

8. ***Educating for global citizenship*** facilitates the awareness of an individual's role in the global ecology, which includes the human family and all other systems of the Earth and universe. Human experience is vastly wider than any single culture's values or ways of thinking. Global education engenders respect for diversity.

9. Humanity requires a healthy planet on which to learn and grow. ***Educating for Earth literacy*** implies an awareness of planetary interdependence, the congruence of personal and global well-being, and the individual's role and scope of responsibility for living in harmony with the natural world.

10. ***Spirituality*** is a deep connection to self and others, a sense of meaning and purpose in daily life, an experience of the wholeness and interdependence of life, and a respite from the activity, pressure and over-stimulation of contemporary life.

IIIa

Copy of first letter sent from Mario Montessori (Holland) to Binda Goldsbrough (England)

September 10, 1939

Dear Binda,

Today I received a letter from your father that gave me your address. First of all, I would like to have the material book; send it at once, by the safest means you can find at the moment.

Mammolina is still determined to go to India, and I am of course going with her in case we succeed in finding a means to reach Bombay.

But in times such as these anything may happen. In case the worst arrives and you survive, form a group with a few others – who have Mammolina in their soul . . .

I am telling you this because I trust you implicitly and I know that you – along with a few others – share my soul and its aim and determination to carry out in its purity the idea of Mammolina.

That is, and it must continue to be, as long as life continues to abide in you, your religion and your aim in life. All the rest: family, ambition, love, must be secondary to the great task. Remember that many can love, there are thousands of families in the world, but there is only one means to bring practical help to humanity, and that is possessed by very few people, and you are among these.

. . . I trust to God that you and others – who are our spiritual children – may find in your love and in your intelligence the means of making Mammolina's message and work penetrate mankind's soul.

As to you, Binda, take good care of yourself. Do not let the present mar your mind and your soul; retain that freshness of spirit and that love that are so necessary to carrying out our work.

As ever,

Mario M. Montessori

© Montessori-Pierson Publishing Company, Amsterdam

IIIb

Copy of second letter sent from Mario Montessori (Holland) to Binda Goldsbrough (England)

25/9/39

Dear Binda,

. . . It has been a real privilege to have known you: among those with whom the work has thrown me in contact, you figure among the most lev-el-headed -self-effacing- and efficient personalities I have met – and if God will that there is a possibility of continuing our work, and also, if your murderous eyes will not make a victim of some soldier boy who will provide you with more children than you have already, then my girl, you ought to figure among the most prominent figures in our history. And if ever the Montessori movement will become as rich as the Swedenborg one, your picture will hang on the walls of our largest hall, and your burning eyes will scare the life of anyone who will dare to lecture unprepared or with a critical mind.

Certainly, the work you have started now is very worthwhile and if you have enough material, and sufficient strength, the result ought to be extraordinary. Do not forget the period of "normalization" before beginning with the material: I believe that the whole secret of having or not having success lies in that. Use the exercises of practical life, in the house, in the garden, and exercises of movement, of behavior, of control of movement, of analysis of movement, and of every kind of exercise that will make the child not only master, but also a conscious master, of all its faculties.

Mammolina and I shall be waiting your report. Meanwhile, give our affectionate greetings to your father and mother – if she is with you, and with kindest regards for Madeleine and yourself.

Yours sincerely,

Mario M. Montessori

IV

The following response was written by Dr. Enid Larsen, Assistant Dean,
Endicott College Graduate School.

January 5, 2020

In my multi-role relationship with TIES (administrative, faculty, artist, collegial collaborator), I was engaged with the TIES program at Endicott College from 1998 – 2019, two decades rich with administrative and academic experimentation and exploration. Experimentation and innovation are the essence of the TIES tradition, as they have steadfastly manifested their vision much in the manner that New England poet Mary Oliver describes as 'lifting the hoof of an idea'. Phil Gang and Marsha Snow had a vision, seeded by passion, and they, idea by idea, step by step, built it into a viable, innovative, transformative pathway for adult learners who don't find their fit or passion in traditional higher education programming.

TIES emerged during a dynamic period in Endicott College history, at a time of receptivity to non-traditional growth and when experimentation and innovation was 'de rigueur'. Despite challenges of its unique needs and programmatic structure, the TIES program brought a certain vitality to the Endicott offering of curriculum and it was satisfying for the administration and staff to support and witness TIES's emergence and growth. TIES's experimentation became my and Endicott's experimentation – summer residencies, my arts-based seminars that evolved to online delivery, deconstructed semesters and administrative models. TIES is an online pioneer in education, discovering the power of digital communities through the simplicity and beauty of meaningful dialogic relationships. Each year seemed to bring yet another consideration, an experiment, upgrade or innovation.

My experience of working with the TIES program was an adventure from the start. It was both our good fortunes that our passion-driven journeys converged - the evolving TIES vision of integrative, holistic, ecological education that honors the interconnectedness between all things in this Universe, and my arts-based autoethnographic research on Eros, passion, and transformation in adult learning. Arts-based researchers envision interconnectedness where criteria are used to identify relationships among areas of interest, rather than a tendency to disaggregate elements into typologies and hierarchies. TIES welcomed our mutual integrative commonalities. Among themes such as Cosmology, Chaos Theory, Ecology, Montessori, Education, Gaia, Autopoiesis, and Integrative Education, arts-based exploration, creativity and passion facilitated a progressive link, first to their own creative capacities, then onward to their individual research interests.

I am deeply touched by the magnitude of standing before the proverbial "blank white page", the "blank canvas", the "clump of clay", and students' latent deep stirrings waiting for expression. Master students, along with most Creatives, lament a range of challenging emotions when they encounter a new project, such as fear, confusion, self-critical and perfectionistic whispers, dis-organized cognition. They are hard put to imagine "lifting the hoof" of their own intelligent inquiry. Here is where the arts began to do their work, albeit first through defamiliarization and exploration with collage and mixed media.

Defamiliarization, a necessity in transformational learning, is an artistic and pedagogical technique to inject a dose of generative disorientation into students' familiar, comfortable, and, perhaps, collective frames of reference. In working with collage and mixed media (with lots of poetry sprinkled through-out), the students bypassed their cogitating minds and bright intellects, essen-tially moving it all aside to dip to deeper levels, into their inner worlds, where one more easily encounter imaginations. Art objects, through their symbolic power, allowed the students to 'try on' or discover different points of view. Imagination and experimentation are closely related, and each encourages the other.

The various steps the students enacted in collage brought meaning-mak-ing into focus: how they chose images, created a composition, connected elements, and attempted to find meaning in the resulting artwork through sharing and dialoging, with each other and with the images. Creative art processes through collage made their experiences and knowledge acquisition tangible, accessible and available for recognition. As one student stated about teaching experiences:

> "I am shocked into the realization that what we seem to have really done is push Love aside – that instead of Love being our guiding principle as we move through our daily experiences, we have been trained to sever or at least discount Love from the majority of the minutes of our days. Krishnamurti (one of our most recent readings) laid the groundwork for this realization in me but for some reason, Eros brought it home."

Through an encounter with their own creative center, the students acquired additional frameworks from which to perceive and respond, enlivened and refreshed, to their personal worlds, master study, and the world at large. Their cognition was expanded, not by traditional structural forms, but by the wisdom of their own instincts, ideas, Eros, and intelligence. As future teachers, leaders, professionals, parents, citizens of the world, does not the world need more of that?

I conclude my sojourn with an over-riding sentiment: The TIES students were, and are, fortunate to participate in TIES's vision of education. The good TIES bring to the world and draws from the students is needed now more than ever. TIES is wonderful and the world needs their perspective, heart-work, hand-work, and educational opportunity.

V

Paul Freedman, President, Self-Design Graduate Institute,
wrote these reflections on TIES.

August 2019

Participating as an assistant mentor in a couple of TIES seminars now has offered me a privileged window through which to witness some of the most personally integrated expressions of study, practice and reflection I have witnessed in education. What is it about TIES that nurtures such authenticity, vulnerability and full presencing among faculty and students alike? There is a depth to the TIES learning encounter that at first blush feels like nothing short of magic. It is indeed the holy grail towards which holistic educators often reach but rarely, if ever, achieve. Upon reflection, however, the mystery of creating this container for depth, presence and authenticity begins to be revealed.

One key component at TIES is the content that is explored. What Parker Palmer would call the "Great Thing" around which the "Community of Truth" gathers. TIES syllabi have the courage and wisdom to seek out what is most important, the very essence of what it means to be human and live well upon this earth. Exploring authors from J Krishnamurti and David Bohm to Margaret Wheatley and Thomas Berry ensure that each seminar is engaging with matters of the utmost weight and import. This is a far cry indeed from typical teacher education programs that might orient around technique, methods and competencies. Courses in traditional education programs, such as "How to Manage Behavior to Maximize Student Achievement" for example, as expected, draw out superficial participation. While common TIES questions around what is "right relationship" in education?, or how can we envision the educational mission to reflect the wisdom of Gaia? or what are the implications of quantum physics on organizational leadership? leads this community to the deepest explorations of soul and spirit, purpose and meaning.

Also critical to TIES success is the expectation and nurturing of students' attention to deep noticing and personal reflection. This is achieved partly by the beautiful "Observation" periods that are sprinkled throughout the M.Ed. program. During these courses, students are encouraged to observe in nature, or as a witness to human encounters. They reflect on what they see, how they feel, and the meaningful implications of these observations. The writing that emerges from students here exudes fullness, vulnerability and sincerity. In a typical post during observations, one student writes:

> I wish I could "be" as freely and easily in other parts of my life as I was observing Blake. Free from worry, demands, timelines, lists-just relaxed pure joy. Being here now without the self imposed pressure. I think that is part of why I love teaching. I am forced to be here now, and be all in.

And this quality of engagement carries easily into seminars, where students' study of new texts and challenging concepts, again is applied to personal lived experiences and reflections on classroom teaching and learning encounters.

A final remarkable and essential element to TIES unique approach, is the quality of the mentors' role and expression. This again bears little-to-no resemblance to the traditional transmission model of higher education, where the faculty lectures, bestowing knowledge upon the passive and receptive learners, *en masse*. At TIES, the faculty open each seminar with such personal and poetic expressions of who they are as human beings, rooted in place and context. They proceed to engage alongside the learners with obvious care, posing key questions in response to students' comments, driving the dialogue ever deeper, in an intricate process known at TIES as "weaving." Often faculty mentors will share new relevant content beyond the syllabus, or add their own reflections, insights and applications of quotes that have been identified by the students. Mentors are willing to expose their own vulnerabilities and not-knowing, always as an invitation to dive deeper together, with awe and wonder. Perhaps most remarkable of all is the mentors' capacity to allow for space and emergence within the dialogue, while still reassuring the community of their watchful caring presence. A common faculty posting is simply, "I am here. Listening and acknowledging. Paying attention."

There is a "quality of being" at TIES, an ontology of presencing, a kind of generative listening that is difficult to describe, but is so clearly and instantly evident. Everything about the program from content to context belies the fact that this work is profoundly important, the individual student is honored and elevated, each person's learning process is recognized and nurtured. TIES' success goes well-beyond method and syllabus. It is a world view, a consciousness that envelopes the program, invading every aspect of the work, like a steady prolonged rainfall seeping into the soil and then slowly occupying a stream bed until all is immersed by the grace and beauty of this holistic learning community of care.

VI

The following reflections were written by Lauren de Boer,
the Founding Editor of EarthLight Magazine, an independent scholar.

September 2, 2019

Ways in which TIES provides the context for personal integration:

1. An extension of the small self into a larger and more dynamic ecological self.

An awareness grows in the TIES experience of the correspondence between one's inner landscape and the landscape of our living planet. A safe and supportive setting is provided wherein a learner can explore the pressure points of one's beliefs without fear of criticism or ridicule. This provides for the cultivation of true critical thinking through introspection and inquiry. The protracted atmosphere of the seminars, allowing for more measured emergence of well-considered ideas, encourages the emergence of this capacity. This allows one to navigate the tensions between the smaller self one inherits from family and culture and the greater Self that calls us to transcend ideology and belief and embrace the larger whole of the cosmic community. While I rarely come into contact with students after they leave the program, I have witnessed the struggle with this tension at times in the seminars. In a couple of instances, with a Catholic and a Muslim participant, there was a palpable process of growth as the course content came into tension, and eventual integration with strongly held beliefs.

2. The nesting of personal story with the larger cosmic story.

To undertake any endeavor, one must have the energy to make the journey. TIES is an energizing program in that it provides a sense of place (ecology) and story (cosmology) as the underpinnings of true learning. One's identity is validated because you see yourself situated within the entire order of living things, not outside. One's sense of purpose is validated because you see yourself situated within a story that is still spinning its narrative from the dynamics of evolution and upon which you can have a direct impact because you are as much the story as every other subject. Out of this comes a felt connection to the energy and will of the planet itself and of the unfolding evolutionary process.

3. Weaving their chosen work with the Great Work of the current era.

The work one brings to the TIES experience is validated because you see that it is integral to the work of the Earth Community, and that it has its purpose in time. In a real sense, the TIES community helps not only plan the garden of learning, but prepares the fertile substratum of the soil. Not until a gardener has spade in hand does the idea of a garden begin to manifest as a verdant and dynamic reality that that produces food and flower. Upon completion of the TIES program, there is a period of waiting for the fruits of one's labor to manifest as the food that sustains and the flower that pollinates and inspires. TIES provides the foundational components to help ensure a successful integration once someone has spade in hand engaging in their work. It's not only the pillars of ecology and cosmology, but the ambit within which they are explored—respectful listening and dialogue and openness to learning as an individual process super-charged by a community of learners. The invocation of the powers of ecology and cosmology provides an energizing matrix within which the human spirit can be adequately prepared for the challenges and difficulties ahead.

REFERENCES

Association Montessori Internationale (2020). *Biography of dr maria montessori.* https://montessori-ami.org/resource-library/facts/biography-dr-maria-montessori \

Australian National University. (2011, September 29). *Cosmic thread that binds us revealed.* Phys.org. http://phys.org/news/2011-09-cosmic-thread-revealed.html#jCp

Bateson, G. (1979/1988). *Mind and nature.* Bantam Books.

Barks, C. (1997). *The essential rumi.* Castle Books.

Bateson, N. (Producer & Director). (2010) *An ecology of mind.* [Motion Picture] United States: Bullfrog Films.

Blum, R. (1990) *The new book of runes.* Retrieved from https://coreyemmah. weebly.com/uploads/2/2/1/8/22181700/blum_-_new_book_of_runes.pdf

Branson, F. (2019, December). *The world is still alive.* The Sun Magazine, Issue 528.

Campbell, Joseph. (1988). *The power of myth.* Doubleday.

Capra, F. (1996) *The web of life: A new scientific understanding of living systems.* Bantam Doubleday.

Capra, F. & Luisi P. L. (2014). *The Systems view of life: A unifying vision.* Cambridge University Press.

Chinmoy, S. (1973) *The dance of life, part 4.* Agni Press. Retrieved from https://www.srichinmoylibrary.com/dl-166

Chinmoy, S. (1995) *The garland of nation-souls: Completed talks at the united nations.* Health Communications.

Chinmoy, S. (1996). *Yoga and the spiritual life.* Aum Publications.

Claremont, C. A. (1920) *Has dr. montessori made a true contribution to science?* Pamphlet. J.E. Francis, Anthenaem Press.

Dass, R. (1975/2019, October 10). *Ram dass – here and now – ep. 152 – the still small voice within* [Audio podcast]. Be Here Now Network. https://beherenow-network.com/ram-dass-here-and-now-ep-152-the-still-small-voice-within

Duncan, D. J. (2014, November) *The unbreakable thread.* The Sun. https://www.thesunmagazine.org/issues/467/the-unbreakable-thread

Huxley, A. (1992). *The divine within.* HarperPerennial.

Easwaran, E. (2007) *The bhagavad gita.* Nilgiri Press.

Edmo, E. (2006). *These few words of mine.* Celilo House, Oregon.

Gandhi, M. (1931, October 28). Speech at Montessori Training College, October 28, 1931, *Young India.* (1931, November19)

Gang, P. S. (1976, April). A School for My Children, *NAMTA Journal.*

Gang, P. and Loew, M. (1981, April 8) *Interview with mario montessori, sr.* [Video] https://vimeo.com/313431426

Gang, P. S. (1989). *Rethinking education.* Dagaz Press.

Hanh, T. N. (1992) *Peace is every step.* Bantam Books.

Hauck, D. (1999). *The emerald tablet: Alchemy for personal transformation.* Penguin Compass.

Huxley, A. (1938) *Ends and means.* Chatto & Windus.

Huxley, A. (1962). *Island* (p. 260). HarperCollins.

Huxley, A. (1992) *The divine within.* HarperPerennial.

Huxley, A. (1944). *Time must have a stop.* Dalkey Archive Press.

Huxley, J. (2014, February 24). *Julian huxley, evolution and meaning.* Reason and Meaning. https://reasonandmeaning.com/2014/02/24/evolutionary-biology-and-the-meaning-of-life/

Huxley, J. (1926). *The stream of life* (p. 56). Watts and Company.

Kahn, D. (1979) *The kodaikanal experience: An interview lena wikramaratne* NAMTA Quarterly V 5/Issue 1 1979.

Krishnamurti, J. (1929, August 3). *Truth is a pathless land.* JKrishnamurti.org. https://jkrishnamurti.org/about-dissolution-speech

Krishnamurti, J. (2015). *Unconditioning and education.* Krishnamurti Foundation of America.

Leone, B. & Montessori, M. (1978) *Knight of the child.* Greenhaven Press.

Maccheroni, A. (1947) *A true romance: Doctor maria montessori as i knew her.* The Darien Press.

MacDonald, D. (2019, May) Personal correspondence.

Malhotra, R. (2014). *Indra's net.* Harper Collins.

McGaa, E. (1991). *Earth prayers.* Harper.

Myers, K. (1913, May 15). *Séguin's principles of education as related to the montessori method.* Journal of Education, Sage Publications.

Montessori, M. Cosmic Education 1935-1936, Lecture I. Communications 2007/1.

Montessori, M. Cosmic Education 1935-1936, Lecture II Communications 2007/2.

Montessori, M. Cosmic Education 1935-1936, Lecture IV Communications 2008/2

Montessori, M. Cosmic Education 1935-1936, Lecture V Communications 2009/1.

Montessori, M. Cosmic Education 1935-1936, Lecture VI Communications 2009/2.

Montessori, M. (1949/1972). *Education and peace*. Henry Regnery Co.

Montessori, M. (1946/1973). *Education for a new world*. Theosophical Publishing House.

Montessori, M. (1955). *Formation of man*. Theosophical Publishing House.

Montessori, M. (1939) *Gandhi and the child*. India News.

Montessori, M. (1942/1973) *Reconstruction in education*. Theosophical Publishing House.

Montessori, M. (1918/1965) *Spontaneous activity in education: The advanced montessori method, vol. 1*, Robert Bentley, Inc.

Montessori, M. (1949) *The absorbent mind*. Kalakshetra Publications.

Montessori, M. (1997) *The california lectures of maria montessori, 1915. Collected speeches & writings. The clio montessori series*. ABC-Clio Ltd.

Montessori, M. (1989). *The child, society and the world*. ABC CLIO.

Montessori, M. (1909, 1912 English). *The montessori method*. Fredrick A. Stokes Company.

Montessori, M. (2013, December). *The White Cross (1917/1918)* AMI Journal 2013/1-2. Amsterdam, The Netherlands.

Montessori, M. (1948/1991). *To educate the human potential.* Kalakshetra Press.

Moretti, E. (2018, March 8). *How to help syria's children.* The Washington Post. https://www.washingtonpost.com/news/made-by-history/wp/2018/03/08/how-to-help-syrias-refugee-children/

Morgan, M. S. (2000). *An ecogenesis for education: A context for learning / perceiving systemic patterns in the design and creation of learning communities* [Unpublished master's thesis]. Vermont College of Norwich University. Retrieved from http://ties-edu.org/gaia/Ecogenesis-for-Education.pdf

Morgan, M. S. & Gang, P. S. (2003) *Interview with brian swimme* [Video]. Vimeo. https://vimeo.com/298046631

Muller, R. (1982). *New genesis.* Doubleday.

Rilke, R. M. (1929/2011). *Letters to a young poet.* Harvard University Press.

Simon, P. https://www.philipsnowgang.net/contact

Schwartzberg, L. (2012, November). *Nature. Beauty. Gratitude.* [Video]. TED Conferences. https://www.ted.com/talks/louie_schwartzberg_nature_beauty_gratitude?language=en

Standing, E.M. (1957). *Maria montessori: Her life and work.* Hollis and Carter Ltd.

Swimme, B. (1984). *The universe is a green dragon: A cosmic creation story.* Bear & Company.

Swimme, B. (2003). www.storyoftheuniverse.org

Teilhard de Chardin, P. (1976). *The phenomenon of man* (p. 265). Harper Perennial.

Trudeau, C. (1984) *Montessori's years in india* [Unpublished doctoral dissertation]. Chaminade University.

Tucker, M. E. & Grim J. (Producers) & Kennard, D. & Northcutt, P. (Directors). (2011) *Journey of the universe* [Motion Picture] United States.

Varela, Francisco, [Gisler, S. (Producer) & Reichle, F. (Director)]. (2005). *Monte grande: What is life?* [Motion Picture]T & C Film AG.

Zohar, D. (1990) *The quantum self.* Quill/William Morrow.

ENDNOTES

Prologue

1   Huxley, A. (1992). *The divine within* (p. 46). HarperPerennial.

2   Montessori, M. (1989). *The child, society and the world* (p. 110). ABC CLIO.

Chapter One

3   Rilke, R. M. (1929/2011). *Letters to a young poet* (p.43). Harvard University Press.

4   Zohar, D. (1990) *The quantum self* (p. 186). Quill/William Morrow.

5   Krishnamurti, J. (2015). *Unconditioning and education* (p. 18). Krishnamurti Foundation of America.

6   Montessori, M. (1949/1972). *Education and peace* (p. 64). Henry Regnery Co.

7   Montessori, M. (1946/1973). *Education for a new world* (p. 13). Theosophical Publishing House.

8   Montessori, M. (1949) *The absorbent mind* (p. 294). Kalakshetra Publications.

Chapter Two

9   Bateson, G. (1979/1988). *Mind and nature* (p. 3). Bantam Books.

10   See https://www.paulsimon.com/track/kodachrome-7/

Chapter Three

11   Australian National University. (2011, September 29). *Cosmic thread that binds us revealed.* Phys.org. http://phys.org/news/2011-09-cosmic-thread-revealed.html#jCp

12   Duncan, D. J. (2014, November) *The unbreakable thread.* The Sun. https://www.thesunmagazine.org/issues/467/the-unbreakable-thread

13   Tucker, M. E. & Grim J. (Producers) & Kennard, D. & Northcutt, P. (Directors). (2011) *Journey of the universe* [Motion Picture] United States.

14   Montessori, M. (1949) *The absorbent mind* (p. 418). Kalakshetra Press.

15   Teilhard de Chardin, P. (1976). *The phenomenon of man* (p. 265). Harper Perennial.

Chapter Four

16   See https://www.dead.net/song/ripple

17   www.storyoftheuniverse.org

18   Varela, Francisco, [Gisler, S. (Producer) & Reichle, F. (Director)]. (2005). *Monte grande: What is life?* [Motion Picture] T & C Film AG.

19   Capra, F. & Luisi P. L. (2014). *The Systems view of life: A unifying vision* (p. 65). Cambridge University Press.

Chapter Five

20   Online dialogue TIES virtual conference "Exploring and Expanding

the Great Work." Title of Elisabet Sahtouris' presentation was *Crisis as Opportunity: An Evolutionary Leap for Humanity*, January 2002.

21   Bateson, N. (Producer & Director). (2010) *An ecology of mind*. [Motion Picture] United States: Bullfrog Films.

22   Gang, P. S. (1976, April). A School for My Children, *NAMTA Journal*.

23   Gang, P. and Loew, M. (1981, April 8) *Interview with Mario Montessori, Sr.* [Video] https://vimeo.com/313431426

24   Swimme, B. (1984). *The universe is a green dragon: A cosmic creation story*. Bear & Company.

Chapter Six

25   Chinmoy, S. (1973) *The dance of life, part 4*. Agni Press. Retrieved from https://www.srichinmoylibrary.com/dl-166

26   21st Montessori Course given by Maria Montessori, London, 1935. (Victoria Goldsbrough's Manuals)

27   Montessori, M. (1948/1991). *To educate the human potential* (p. 7). Kalakshetra Press.

28   13th Montessori Elementary Course, Bergamo, Italy 1973-74. (Philip Snow Gang Manuals)

29   Montessori, M. (1946/1976). *Education for a new world* (p.3). Kalakshetra Press.

30   21st Montessori Course given by Maria Montessori, London, 1935. (Victoria Goldsbrough's Manuals)

31   Huxley, J. (2014, February 24). *Julian huxley, evolution and meaning*. Reason and Meaning. https://reasonandmeaning.com/2014/02/24/evolutionary-biology-and-the-meaning-of-life/

32   Muller, R. (1982). *New genesis* (p. 41). Doubleday.

33   Montessori, M. (1949) *The absorbent mind* (p.286). Kalakshetra Press.

34   ibid, p. 207.

35   Blum, R. (1990) *The new book of runes.* Retrieved from https://co-reyemmah.weebly.com/uploads/2/2/1/8/22181700/blum_-_new_book_of_runes.pdf

36   Easwaran, E. (2007) *The bhagavad gita* (p. 17). Nilgiri Press.

37   Huxley, A. (1944). *Time must have a stop* (p. 248). Dalkey Archive Press.

38   Huxley, A. (1992) *The divine within* (p. 46). HarperPerennial.

Chapter Seven

39   Morgan, M. S. (2000). *An ecogenesis for education: A context for learning / perceiving systemic patterns in the design and creation of learning communities* [Unpublished master's thesis]. (p. 4). Vermont College of Norwich University. Retrieved from http://ties-edu.org/gaia/Ecogenesis-for-Education.pdf

40   Kermani, V. (2017, April 19). *What modern ecology can learn from ancient hinduism.* https://www.ecologise.in/2017/04/19/what-modern-ecology-can-learn-from-ancient-hinduism/

41   Prime, R. (2004) *Vedic ecology: Practical wisdom for surviving the 21st century* (p. 24). Mandala Publishing.

42   10th Montessori Elementary Course, Bergamo, Italy 1970-71. (Mario Montessori Lecture)

43   See https://www.ties-edu.org/our-planet-our-home/ for more information on these materials.

44   Capra, F., & Luisi, P. L. (2014). *The systems view of life: A unifying vision* (p. 352). Cambridge University Press.

45   Morgan, M. S. (2000) *An ecogenesis for education: A context for learning / Perceiving systemic patterns in the design and creation of learning communities* [Unpublished master's thesis]. (p. 14). Vermont College of Norwich University. Retrieved from http://ties-edu.org/gaia/Ecogenesis-for-Education.pdf

Chapter Eight

46   Link to author's video, *Peace through education* [Video]. https://vimeo.com/245042969

47   Hanh, T. N. (1992) *Peace is every step* (p. 38). Bantam Books.

48   Krishnamurti, J. (1929, August 3). *Truth is a pathless land.* JKrishnamurti.org. https://jkrishnamurti.org/about-dissolution-speech

49   Muller, R. (1982). *New genesis* (p. 89). Doubleday.

50   Montessori, M. (2013, December). *The White Cross (1917/1918)* AMI Journal 2013/1-2, pp. 37-41 Amsterdam, The Netherlands.

51   Moretti, E. (2018, March 8). *How to help syria's children.* The Washington Post. https://www.washingtonpost.com/news/made-by-history/wp/2018/03/08/how-to-help-syrias-refugee-children/

52   Gandhi, M. (1931, October 28). Speech at Montessori Training College, October 28, 1931, *Young India.* (1931, November19)

53   Krishnamurti, J. (1974). *Unconditioning and education, Vol 1* (p. 15). Krishnamurti Foundation Trust Ltd.

54   Nandakumar, A. (2017). Graduate Review Submission

55   Jones, A. (2017). Graduate Review Submission

56   Capra, F. (1996) *The web of life: A new scientific understanding of living*

systems (p. 36). Bantam Doubleday.

57   Hijazi, H. (2017). Graduate Review Submission

58   Chinmoy, S. (1995) *The garland of nation-souls: Completed talks at the united nations.* (p.78). Health Communications.

59   Nandakumar, A. (2017). Graduate Review Submission

60   Smith M. (2017). Graduate Review Submission

61   Montessori, M. (1939) *Gandhi and the child.* India News.

Chapter Nine

62   21st Montessori Course, London, 1935. (Victoria Goldsbrough's manuals)

63   Montessori, M. (1946/1989) *The child, society and the world.* (p.110, 1946 lecture in India). ABC CLIO.

64   Montessori uses the term Children's House (*Casa dei Bambini* in Italian) to refer to a classroom of children ranging from 2.5 to 6 years of age.

65   Montessori, M. Cosmic Education 1935-1936, Lecture VI Communications 2009/2 (p. 40).

66   Montessori, M. Cosmic Education 1935-1936, Lecture I Communications 2007/1 (p. 57).

67   Leone, B. & Montessori, M. (1978) *Knight of the child.* (p. 12). Greenhaven Press.

68   ibid (p. 15).

69   Maccheroni, A. (1947) *A true romance: Doctor maria montessori as i knew her* (p.11). The Darien Press.

70   Standing, E.M. (1957). *Maria montessori: Her life and work* (p. 25).

Hollis and Carter Ltd.

71   ibid (p.31)

72   ibid (p. 31)

73   Maccheroni, A. (1947). *A true romance: Doctor maria montessori as i knew her* (p. 7). The Darien Press.

74   Association Montessori Internationale (2020). *Biography of dr maria montessori.* https://montessori-ami.org/resource-library/facts/biography-dr-maria-montessori

75   In that time these children were referred to as feeble-minded, defective, or retarded.

76   Association Montessori Internationale (2020). *Biography of dr maria montessori.* https://montessori-ami.org/resource-library/facts/biography-dr-maria-montessori

77   Myers, K. (1913, May 15). *Séguin's principles of education as related to the montessori method.* Journal of Education, Sage Publications.

78   During the first period *(This is...)* the teacher names the quality or object and makes the necessary associations. In the second period *(Show me...)* the teacher still furnishes the name, but the child must recognize it. In the third *(What is this?)* children actually verbalize what they have learned.

79   Montessori, M. (1909/1970). *The Montessori Method* (1909, 1912 English) as cited in *Montessori: A centenary anthology* (1970, p. 10).

80   Huxley, A. (1938) *Ends and means,* (pp. 181-2). Chatto & Windus. [The pamphlet he quotes from was *Education and Peace* published by the International Office of Education (Geneva, 1932 and included as Chapter 1 in Montessori's 1949 book of the same title). How would Huxley come upon this obscure printing? *Authors note:* It was also published in various

booklets, and widely promoted, so he may easily have found one. He may actually have attended one of Montessori's lectures, probably at the European Congress for Peace (1936, Brussels).]

81   Montessori, M. (1909, 1912 English). *The montessori method* (p.9). Fredrick A. Stokes Company.

82   ibid (p. 374)

83   ibid (p. 375)

84   Montessori, M. (1989). *The child, society and the world* (p. 93) ABC CLIO.

85   Huxley, J. (1926). *The stream of life* (p. 56). Watts and Company.

86   Claremont, C. A. (1920) *Has dr. montessori made a true contribution to science?* Pamphlet. J.E. Francis, Anthenaem Press.

87   Having observed the younger child in the indoor and outdoor (natural) environments, and viewed the traits of normalization, Montessori did go on to find ways to present these concepts to older children, but that did not happen until she was in India.

88   Montessori, M. Cosmic Education 1935-1936, Lecture I Communications 2007/1 (p. 56).

89   Montessori, M. (1948). *To educate the human potential* (p. 50). Kalakshetra Press.

90   Montessori, M. Cosmic Education 1935-1936, Lecture V Communications 2009/1 (p. 34).

91   Montessori, M. Cosmic Education 1935-1936, Lecture II Communications 2007/2 (p. 5).

92   Montessori, M. Cosmic Education 1935-1936, Lecture V Communications 2009/1 (p. 33).

93   Good examples of this are Victoria Goldsbrough's (unpublished)1935 hand-written Montessori Teaching Manuals. She was an English speaker and took her notes from what the translator repeated while Montessori lectured. Although accuracy is approached, it can not be guaranteed.

94   Montessori at first borrows from Stoppani and uses "Telluric" economy to refer to the integration of geological functions on Earth. She later calls it the "cosmic economy." Today we would say the Gaian economy or the Gaian cycles.

95   Montessori, M. Cosmic Education 1935-1936, Lecture IV Communications 2008/2 (p. 56)

96   ibid (p. 58)

97   As soon as humans used tools, perhaps two million years ago, they began the ascent to supra-humanity, a species that has the ability to impose its will on nature… at least in the short arc of geological history.

98   Montessori, M. Cosmic Education 1935-1936, Lecture VI Communications 2009/2 (p. 41).

99   International Montessori Conference, Amsterdam, The Netherlands, April 1950, unpublished proceedings.

100   MacDonald, D. (2019, May) Personal correspondence.

101   Montessori, M. (1949) *The absorbent mind* (p. 270). Kalakshetra Publications.

102   Montessori, M. (1997) *The california lectures of maria montessori, 1915. Collected speeches & writings. The clio montessori series* (p.246). ABC-Clio Ltd.

103   Montessori, M. (1949) *The absorbent mind* (p. 291). Kalakshetra Publications.

104   ibid (p. 294)

105   ibid (p. 296)

106   ibid (p. 207)

107   Although Gibran's book, *The Prophet*, was published in 1923, I do not know if Montessori had a copy of it before she went to India or whether it was acquired while she was living there.

108   Montessori, M. (1948/1973) *To educate the human potential* (p. 9). Kalakshetra Press.

109   ibid (p .9)

110   Trudeau, C. (1984) *Montessori's years in india* [Unpublished doctoral dissertation]. (p. 86). Chaminade University.

111   ibid (pp. 86-7)

112   Kahn, D. (1979) *The kodaikanal experience: an interview Lena Wikramaratne* NAMTA Quarterly V 5/Issue 1 1979. pp. 45-53.

113   The information for these stories is written in *To Educate the Human Potential*. Mario shared the creation story, *God with No Hands,* as a "gift from his mother" to the students at *Centro Internazionale Studi Montessoriani* (Bergamo, Italy). It is a blend of mystery and science. People who worked with Mario later developed the other Great Lessons.

114   Malhotra, R. (2014). *Indra's net* (p. 14). Harper Collins.

115   As cited *Centro Internazionale Studi Montessoriani,* Bergamo, Italy, 1973-1974. *Time Line of Life - Level III: The Cosmic Work.*

116   Montessori, M. (1942/1973) *Reconstruction in education* (p. 14). Theosophical Publishing House.

117   In this book, Montessori introduces the term *absorbent mind* for the

first time.

118   Montessori, M. (1946/1973) *Education for a new world* (p. 13). Theosophical Publishing House.

119   Montessori, M. (1955). *Formation of man* (p. 14). Theosophical Publishing House.

120   ibid (p. 18)

121   ibid (pp. 45-6)

122   Kramer, R. (1976) *Maria montessori* (p. 342) G.P. Putnam's Sons.

123   Montessori, M. (1989) *The child, society and the world* (p. 108). ABC CLIO (Note on the use of Ahinahita: Author's research found that Anahita is an ancient Persian goddess. https://www.ancient.eu/Anahita/)

124   Chinmoy, S. (1996). *Yoga and the spiritual life* (p. 47). Aum Publications.

125   Perennial philosophy (2020, May 14). In *Wikipedia.* https://en.wikipedia.org/wiki/Perennial_philosophy

126   Montessori, M. (1949/1972). *Education and peace* (p.55). Henry Regnery Company.

127   Montessori, M. (1989). *The child, society and the world* (p. 99) ABC CLIO.

Chapter Ten

128   Adapted from: Gang, P. S. (2016, August 8). *To educate eco-sapiens* [Video]. Vimeo. https://vimeo.com/178044426

129   Campbell, Joseph. (1988). *The power of myth* (p. xvi). Doubleday.

130   Edmo, E. (2006). *These few words of mine.* Celilo House, Oregon.

131   Krishnamurti, J. (2015). *Unconditioning and education* (p. 63). Krishnamurti Foundation of America.

132   Morgan, M. S. & Gang, P. S. (2003) *Swimme interview* [Video]. Vimeo. https://vimeo.com/298046631

133   Montessori, M. (1948). *To educate the human potential* (p. 15). Kalakshetra Publications.

134   ibid (p.28)

135   Ibid. (p. 41)

136   A communal ritual in which participants step aside from their human identity and speak on behalf of another life-form.

137   Barks, C. (1997). *The essential rumi.* Castle Books.

138   Campbell, J. (1988). *Power of myth.* Doubleday.

139   McGaa, E. (1991). *Earth prayers* (p. 119). Harper.

140   Gang, P. S. (1989). *Rethinking dducation* (p 22). Dagaz Press.

141   ibid (p.37)

142   An approach to innovation that seeks sustainable solutions to human challenges by emulating nature's time-tested patterns and strategies. (biomimicry.org)

Chapter Eleven

143   In a 1939 lecture at London Montessori identifies the "Four Planes of Education," but the term *development* was used in 1950 lectures at Perugia.

144   He was also part of the Dutch resistance during WWII, hiding people in his home. The Nazis arrested him in 1944, and he was murdered in January, 1945.

145   Margaret Drummond read the article at the Montessori Society Open Meeting, held in connection with the Conference of Educational Association, University College London. The chairman was H.R. Hamley, professor of education at the University of London. The article was published by the Maria Montessori Training Organisation in London, 1939 in the Bulletin of the International Montessori Association, year 2, nr 1, p. 27-36. It was later included in the appendix to *From Childhood to Adolescence*, published in 1948.

146   Morgan, M. S. (2000) *An ecogenesis for education: A context for learning / Perceiving systemic patterns in the design and creation of learning communities* [Unpublished master's thesis]. Vermont College of Norwich University. Retrieved from http://ties-edu.org/gaia/Ecogenesis-for-Education.pdf

147   Branson, F. (2019, December). *The world is still alive*. The Sun Magazine, Issue 528, pp.5-21.

148   ibid

149   *Tertiary* refers to the whole field of adult education including undergraduate and graduate studies.

150   Morgan, M. S. (2000) *An ecogenesis for education: A context for learning / Perceiving systemic patterns in the design and creation of learning communities* [Unpublished master's thesis]. Vermont College of Norwich University. Retrieved from http://ties-edu.org/gaia/Ecogenesis-for-Education.pdf

151   A Montessori material containing 27 prisms and cubes that represents $(a + b + c)^3 = a^3 + b^3 + c^3 + 3a^2b + 3a^2c + 3b^2a + 3b^2c + 3c^2a + 3c^2b + 6abc$

152   Ten cubes, pink in color, graduated from 1 cm^3 through 10 cm^3

153   The ability to connect with and speak of the issues from a non-conceptual, bodily-felt experience.

154   Montessori, M. (1948/1991). *To educate the human potential*. Kalak-

shetra Press.

155   Montessori, M. (1918/1965) *Spontaneous activity in education: The advanced montessori method, vol. 1*, Robert Bentley, Inc.

156   During personal discussions with Mario Montessori, Jr., at his home in Amsterdam, he told me quite emphatically that those words were first spoken by him as a child, and then his grandmother used him as an example when explaining her approach.

157   10th Montessori Elementary Course, Bergamo, Italy 1970-71. (Mario Montessori Lecture)

Chapter Twelve

158   Chinmoy, S. (1996). *Yoga and the spiritual life* (p.32). Aum Publications.

159   Hauck, D. (1999). *The emerald tablet: Alchemy for personal transformation* (p. 131). Penguin Compass.

160   Huxley, A. (1962). *Island* (p. 260). HarperCollins.

161   Montessori, M. (1949). *The absorbent mind* (p. 2). Kalakshetra Publications.

Chapter Thirteen

162   Dass, R. (1975/2019, October 10). *Ram dass – here and now – ep. 152 – the still small voice within* [Audio podcast]. Be Here Now Network. https://beherenownetwork.com/ram-dass-here-and-now-ep-152-the-still-small-voice-within/

163   Swimme, B. *Powers of the universe: Episode 11, Radiance*. Retrieved from https://storyoftheuniverse.org/store-2/dvd/the-powers-of-the-universe/

164   ibid

165   Schwartzberg, L. (2012, November). *Nature. Beauty. Gratitude.* [Video]. TED Conferences. https://www.ted.com/talks/louie_schwartzberg_nature_beauty_gratitude?language=en

166   Morgan, M. S. & Gang, P. S. (2003) *Interview with brian swimme* [Video]. Vimeo. https://vimeo.com/298046631

Appendix

167   This is a 1996 condensation and adaptation of the 1991 original. Original may be found at: https://www.ties-edu.org/wp-content/uploads/2020/01/2020_GATE-2000.pdf

INDEX

A

The Absorbent Mind (Montessori), 21, 79, 126

Adolescence: An Exploration (AMI International Study Conference), 63

adolescent education, 63, 136, 145

adults, Montessori for. See TIES (Institute for Educational Studies)

Ahinahita, 133

AHP (Association for Humanistic Psychology), 69

Aikido, 157

AMI (Association Montessori Internationale), 62, 65

Aristotle, 88

Arundale, George, 123

Athena, 16

atmosphere in partnership function, 91, 94

attraction
    as autopoiesis, 45
    love and, 48

B

D

G

O

P